We stood with our feet firmly planted on the hot, hard pebbles of the Southernmost tip of Africa. The Great Waters of the Indian and Atlantic Oceans collide in front of us before rumbling towards the South Pole. Four intrepid individuals, our paths crisscrossing to deposit us here, a special and almost sacred spot for all South Africans. Many of us journey from far and wide to be able to say.... we have stood at the Southernmost tip of this beautiful and wild continent we call home.

My son was on his way to America, his birthplace and I was there to sever the invisible strings that had held us together for so long. It was the most appropriate way I could find to say goodbye. I knew he would not return, bar an occasional visit.

So with the wind whipping about us and without a word, I released a part of my heart. We took a photo as a reminder of this momentous occasion. I captured the image for Ramblings, which is as much a story of my son as it is of myself.

-Anita Bunn

Published by **Magic Rabbit Pty Ltd**
Rosenhof Farms, Annandale Road, Lynedoch, 7603

First published 2021

Publication © Magic Rabbit Pty Ltd

Text © Anita Bunn 2021

All artwork © Anita Bunn

All pencil sketches © Selma Leach

Publishing Manager: Anita Bunn

Cover Design: Anita Bunn

Text Design and Typesetting: Olivia Battani

Fonts used: Baskerville Old Face, Bell MT, Bodoni MT & Arboria

Reproduction by Print On Demand

ISBN: 9780620946773

Table of Contents

Foreword...3

Thank You's...5

Dedications...7

CHAPTER 1 - Genesis...9

CHAPTER 2 - Unintentional Happenings..15

CHAPTER 3 - My Winging Attitude or Not.....................................19

CHAPTER 4 - Harvest Time..23

CHAPTER 5 - Traditions...27

CHAPTER 6 - Foraging..29

CHAPTER 7 - Roger...35

CHAPTER 8 -The Tortoise Crossing & When Shit Happens.........39

CHAPTER 9 - Da Case of Da Sibling..45

CHAPTER 10 - Making the Most...51

CHAPTER 11 - Down Under with My Sister....................................57

CHAPTER 12 - The Prince..61

CHAPTER 13 - When Things Get Weird..69

CHAPTER 14 - New Chapters to be Written....................................73

Glossary of Terms...79

Foreword

One of the greatest privileges, and joys, of my life's journey has been meeting many astounding women, who represent strength, courage, independence, resourcefulness, generosity and resilience. Women who exemplify the power of love, and exhibit tolerance and respect for all living beings, and embrace the opportunities contained in every day, every season, every encounter.

My beautiful friend Anita encapsulates life in all its manifestations... her world is bursting at the seams, literally and figuratively. She is the salt of the earth, glorious and vibrant - represented by her garden (and kitchen) of abundance, which feeds body and soul of all who enter through her blue door. Stepping into her world is like immersing oneself in a canvas of vibrant colour, texture, flavour and scent - and she unhesitatingly shares the fruits of her labour, delighting in the embrace of kindred spirits, unhesitatingly taking those in need under her ample wings... and to be a part of her menagerie of friends, family, animals, and all green living things under her tender care, is to know the force that is her very being.

Over the many years I've known Anita, her versatility became more and more evident, and upon entering through her portal, I would observe her in the midst of one or another creative endeavor, whether standing in front of a huge canvas, glass of wine in one hand, paintbrush in the other, classical music pouring out of the cottage and drifting over the vineyards, as she captured scenes of whimsy or fantasy, in flamboyant colors and brushstrokes, expressing mystical depictions akin to folklore, or renditions of her countless experiences and encounters with humans, animals and plant-life, or picturesque dreamscapes. Always, I would recognize characters from her journey, and marvel at the creativity of her spirit.

Her writing has always been the same, a free-flowing narrative, a gorgeous tumbling of words and observations and exclamations, so often introducing me to colloquialisms and vernacular so particular to this beautiful country on the southern tip of Africa, with its diversity of peoples, culture, languages and lifestyles. In the cascade of words, she captures the embers of life as she embraces it, wholeheartedly, impassioned, unapologetic and eloquent, and always with that magic ingredient of humour, and insight into humanity's soul.

To eat a meal at her table is to experience a splendid, if somewhat chaotic, culinary joyride. Almost every component is home-grown, or raised, by her, and her open shelves groan with the weight of preserves of every kind imaginable (and on one catastrophic occasion, the whole burdened top shelf came down with a resounding crash, taking with it – on the way down – the two lower shelves containing all her precious crockery, from wedding gift sets to other sentimental items collected over years).

So she returned home to a sticky mess that defied description, but true to her resilient nature, she simply rolled up her sleeves, gave a universal shrug of "oh well, these things happen!", and got on with cleaning up the mess. And then started cooking and pickling and preserving the next installment, which as I write, is again on a top shelf groaning and buckling under the weight, with the next generation of crockery precariously perched below.

Anita is indeed the spice of life, and embraces each day as if it were the most precious gift. She loves unreservedly, and knows full well that the price of love, so often, is grief. And yet she remains dauntless, her credo could well be, "Bring it on..."

- Carolyn Frost –Editor, Bolander

Thank You's

I owe my adventures to everyone around me. A deep thank you to all my interesting and sometimes weird friends whom contributed to my journey thus far. My friends and family that understand me and sometimes pretend to understand me but love me unconditionally.

A big fat thank you to my delightful son Roger. Without him life would not have taken its many paths and would not have been such a learning curve. And it probably would not have been so meaningful. I am so glad you did decide to exit my tummy. 9 days late mind you.

I have been blessed with so many strong women in my life. A gazillion one hundred thousand and ten million thank you's to each and every one of you. You have made it pretty easy to write all these tales.

A huge and in my heart thank you to my man, Peter. He is my alter ego as much as I am his. Peas in a pod. Thank you for always giving my ideas and crazy meanderings a chance. Thank you for always helping out with the execution of some wild rides. Thank you mostly, for showing me what a man should be like and what real love is.

Carolyn, gifted writer and pure friend...thank you

Selma, what an artist you are. Your exquisite pencil drawings capture every essence of my stories. Dankie, my vriendin.

Olivia, thank you so much for being my son's partner and helping with the practical stuff of publishing which I absolutely detest and know fuckall about.

A great big fat hug and thank you to Naulene Evans for patiently teaching me the intricacies of the publishing world.

And the last thank you to all of my animals that have taught me so much about life.

Anita Bunn

Take care of this earth.

Just a small wee disclaimer: half of the people in this book are imaginary and the other half are not.

This book is dedicated to all those intrepid souls that beat their own
drum, to those that know their own worth: blood, sweat, tears
and all. Fuck yes!

To Tannie Alda, Mother to Many. Sonder Tannie was ons net
Kinders van die Wind- Koos du Plessis
(Without you, we were just Children of the Wind.)

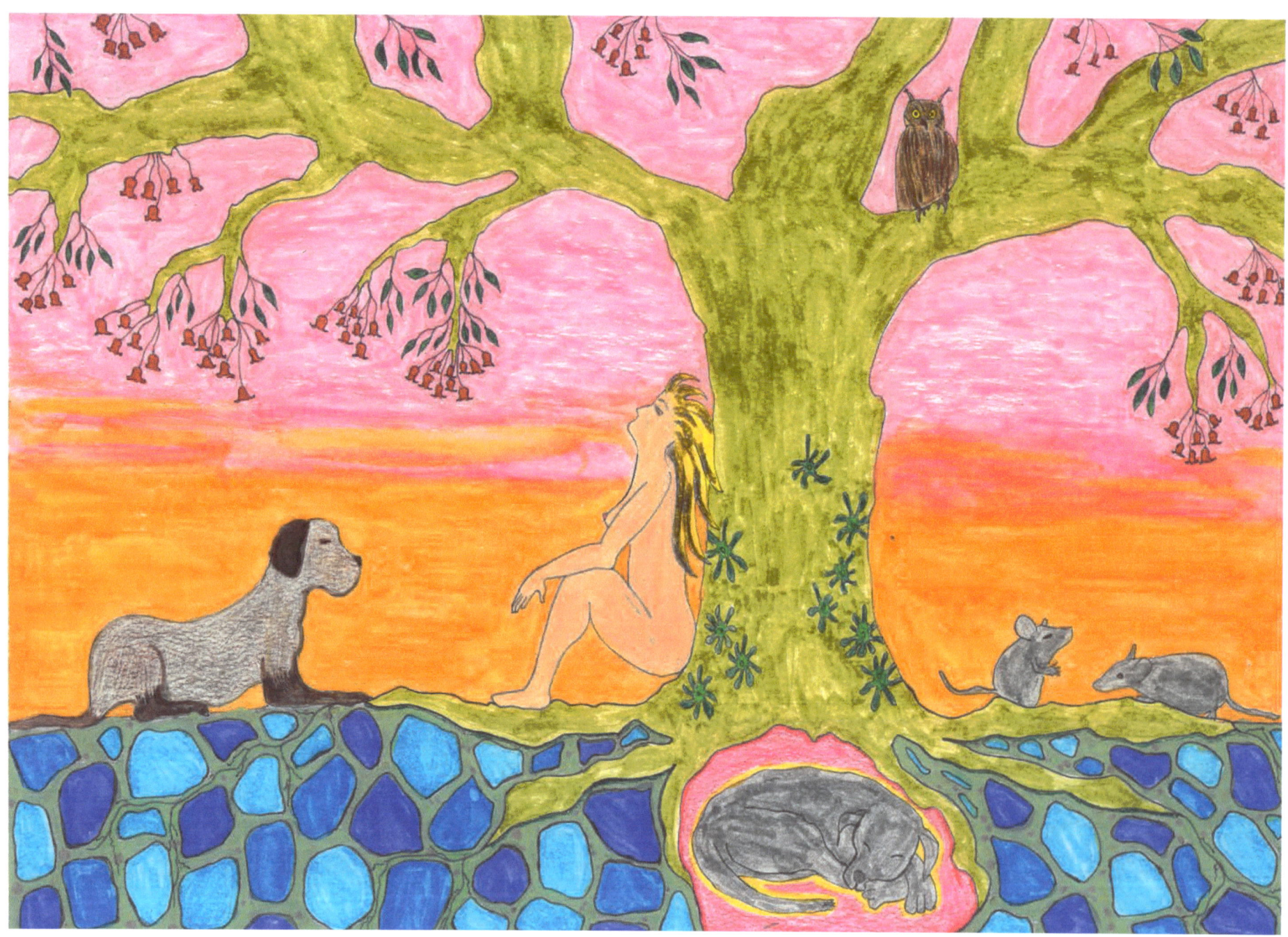

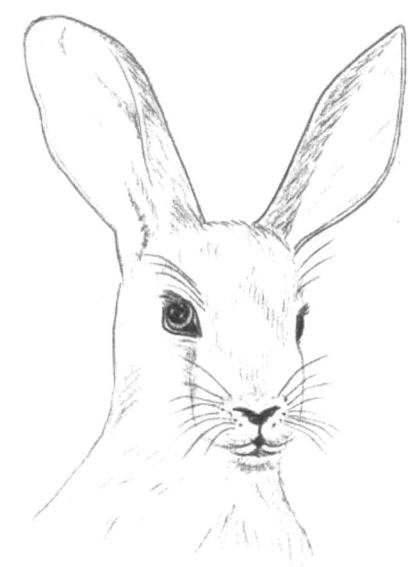

1
GENESIS

I was an odd child, oblivious of my penchant for eccentricity, happy and adventurous with a keen interest in animals and all things green.

Clueless would probably be kind. Absolutely clueless, and so a life heavily weighing on instinct and spontaneity, which one was at that precise minute in play would never be known and whether they were actually masquerading as each other. Well.... Can I start my story of a life in Africa?

I am blessed with a bad memory, which in life is not such a bad thing – as horrible hurts are soon forgotten, and the next adventure awaits. But does it make writing difficult? Fuck yes. Fortunately, I penned some stories in my life, so instead of writing chronologically about my many adventures, I will tell the tales at random – and hopefully confuse you for the worse part, and entertain you for the best part.

These tales will be fraught with grammatical errors and a few spelling mistakes, but heaps of laughter (I fervently hope) and candor will spill forth and hopefully not drown anyone.

I moved to a little cottage on a huge farm in the middle of the Stellenbosch wine country 25 years ago. Just by accident, I met someone who knew someone who lived on a neighbouring farm, and after a party I decided that that is where I would love to raise my son.... nope, did not happen that way.

I just liked the idea of freedom...nope.... I just spontaneously decided my son and I must move to the farm. There was no real thought pattern involved, hours of introspection......uhuh. Just a spur of the moment decision, which then had a humongous impact on my life and my son's development.

One single decision. And it sets you on a path of no return, but with many meanderings and an occasional halt.
It was a small cottage, dilapidated, with a single palm tree and some Shasta daisies[1]. No fences.

25 years back it was the most irresponsible thing to do. A woman... Alone with a 2 year-old-son. I was not very popular with my mom. Thinking back today, I know that it could not have been any other way, as my whole childhood was a warm-up to this.

I grew up in a small suburb which was still under construction, about 14km outside of a medium-sized city, Port Elizabeth. There were about 20 houses with no infrastructure, no shops, mostly gravel roads, with a beautiful estuary as one border, the sea as another and the endless bush of the Eastern Cape. Paradise. We ran wild.

Went where we wanted to, and came home often too late. Our lives were not complete without dogs, ducks, snakes, wild buck, and the longest and biggest earthworms in the world. It surely was a carefree childhood. Alternate holidays we would visit my mom's very large (in all ways) family.

The headquarters was Rietfontein, my mom's sister and her family. Uncle Dave farmed with mostly corn and sunflowers, but kept pigs, sheep, cattle and at one stage a magnificent black horse, the name now escapes me.

When we arrived, most of the family would already be there. It was a kissing and hugging business which I escaped cunningly, as my first visit had to be the animals. I just had to go and say hello and always found the farm folk slaughtering their Xmas pig and sheep.

I could not get enough of this ritual and would watch in awe, the ease of their movements as they disembowelled the animal. This fascination with the ritual of slaughtering would extend through my entire life.

My uncle would grow cash crops, which had to be picked early and transported to the market on the same day, and I relished this necessity. I was the first to start picking in the dark, and drove with my uncle in his huge lorry[2]. I am sure there were other people who came with us, but in my mind, I can only remember Uncle Dave and myself.

I absolutely adored the farm. It was not easy making a living as the farm had been subdivided, but as a child I was oblivious to my uncle and aunt's struggles.

So, this is the background of the woman who decided on a whim that a small cottage on a large farm would be the ideal place to live.
I was a carefree mother, and had a singularly unusual attitude about rearing a child. I was strict with beginsels[3], as an example when my son was about 12 or so, he went through a phase where he would lie to me. Now a lie is equivalent to someone slapping me thru the face with a large snoek[4] .

So, after many sermons on the virtues of truth, and especially between two people living their lives so closely together as the two of us were, Roger came with yet another lie.

We never had money, always scraping along, so a R250 Toys-r-Us voucher was a big thing for my son. I looked at him and asked him to bring the voucher and a pair of scissors. I glared at him with my I-have-had-it-with-this-lying-stuff stare, and said that he has to learn the repercussions of lying.

I cut the voucher into pieces. As I say, I was strict in certain ways, but very lenient and flexible in all other aspects of our lives. My son had a voice and could change my mind. Which he often did. He had freedom to explore a huge farm, had responsibilities towards animals, and a mother who suffered from serious migraines and always worked full days.

So, when I found a family with a son the same age as Roger not far away, whom had just suffered the brutal murder of the boy's mother, it was the beginning of a wonderful adventure for these two boys whom soon became inseparable. I started gardening around our little cottage, adding a garden here and there, anywhere. The soil was hard and unforgiving. My little patch had been used as a scrap yard, which was wonderful for two little boys – but not so good to establish gardens on no budget.

Without one minute of thought, I said yes to pigs and chickens, ducks, dogs, snakes, rats, cats, rabbits, a pet lamb, a cockatiel, and so forth. All this while rearing a child and working full time. I did have boundless energy, with a strong belief in the now. It never occurred to me to wonder about the things that could go wrong. Not one moment was spent on that pursuit.

I was a creative woman, delving into painting, and writing occasionally. Never taking anything seriously... ok, I may have a problem focusing on one thing.

My friend was an editor for a community paper and she kindly allowed some writing to be published in her newspaper. Wacky tales of our life on the farm, tips on gardening which may or may not have been so accurate. One of my first short stories was about my garden.

AUTUMN TIPTOES IN BOLANDER, 25 MARCH 2009

One of my core beliefs in establishing and maintaining a vegetable garden is manure, manure, manure! Oh, how I can wax on lyrically about the virtues of manure. Not only do the animals we keep nourish us, but they supply us with mounds and mounds of glorious manure.

I am lucky enough to have a friend, Willem, who supplies me with rather exotic manure. Not mere cow manure. Oh no, the manure he so graciously gives to me consists of none other than Llama poop, bambi poop, donkey poop, ostrich poop and sturdy Dexter poop. Black gold, I say, black gold!

Sometimes, as in this summer, I get hold of some cow manure from the farm I live on and surprise, surprise, pumpkins all over the show. What a bonus. One year I even had stinging nettles. The lesson to be learned: "Know your cow". My best birthday gift, a bakkie[5] load of manure – what can I say. Editor's Note: Since this article was written in 2009 when I was still largely ignorant on the principles of composting, I ended up with unpleasant results. So no, not know your cow! Additionally, poorly composted manure i.e., green manure, will lead to nitrogen loss in your plants, with the manure competing with your plants for nitrogen.

So, this time of year is the silly season. It's hot, you've harvested, and everything is looking tired. Time for a clean-up. Pull out all the tired-looking plants, add as much manure as you can put your grubby little hands on and allow the soil to rest and the manure to break down.

Editor's Note: Subsequently, I have learned the value of composting.

This rest period may be a month – I do believe the soil must rest. It is still hot enough for the manure to break down, and come autumn, perfect conditions.

In my garden at this time of year, peace reigns. The land I used for my corn is resting. My aubergines, chillies and green peppers are bravely pressing on: my lettuces, spring onions and green beans are always growing, no matter the season, but the pumpkins, cucumbers, tomatoes and melons and butternuts are out. Editor's Note: Green beans do not do well in winter. Another hard lesson.

I have seeded some carrots and planted some peas (yes, a bit early). Editor's Note: Not really, autumn being the perfect time to plant peas.

Just low key, just ticking over, but mostly things are resting.

The frenetic pace of the summer is over, the tempo is slowing down. The slight chill in the morning air is evidence of the slow changing of the season. How incredible, barely noticeable. Here and there, vine leaves are turning autumn red. Enjoy this slower pace, enjoy the winding down, enjoy the essence of the last summer rays.

Anita Bunn lives on a piece of paradise near Stellenbosch, surrounded by pot-bellied pigs, ducks, geese, chickens and a collection of cats and dogs (including three Great Danes). Art and gardening are her passions.

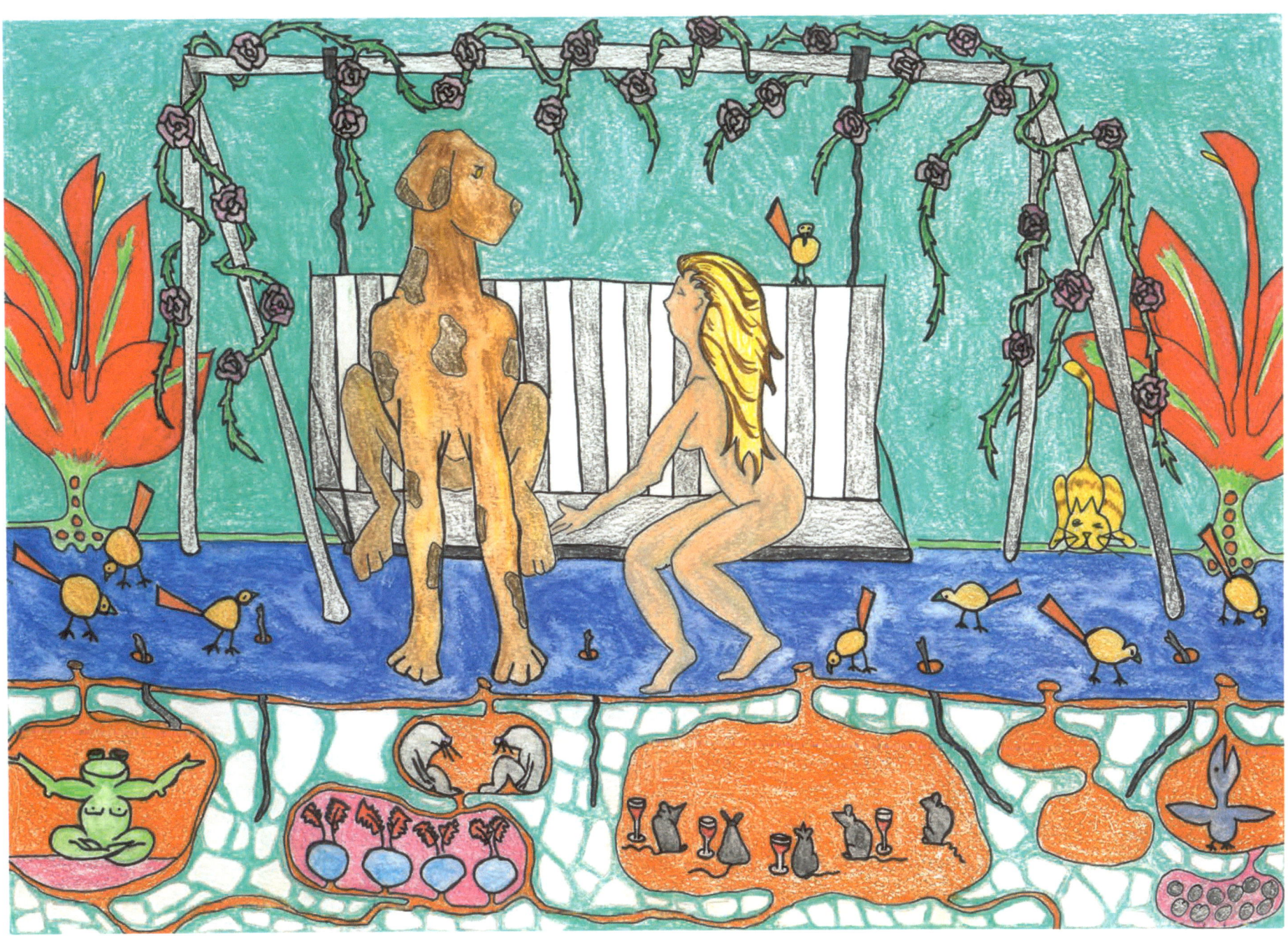

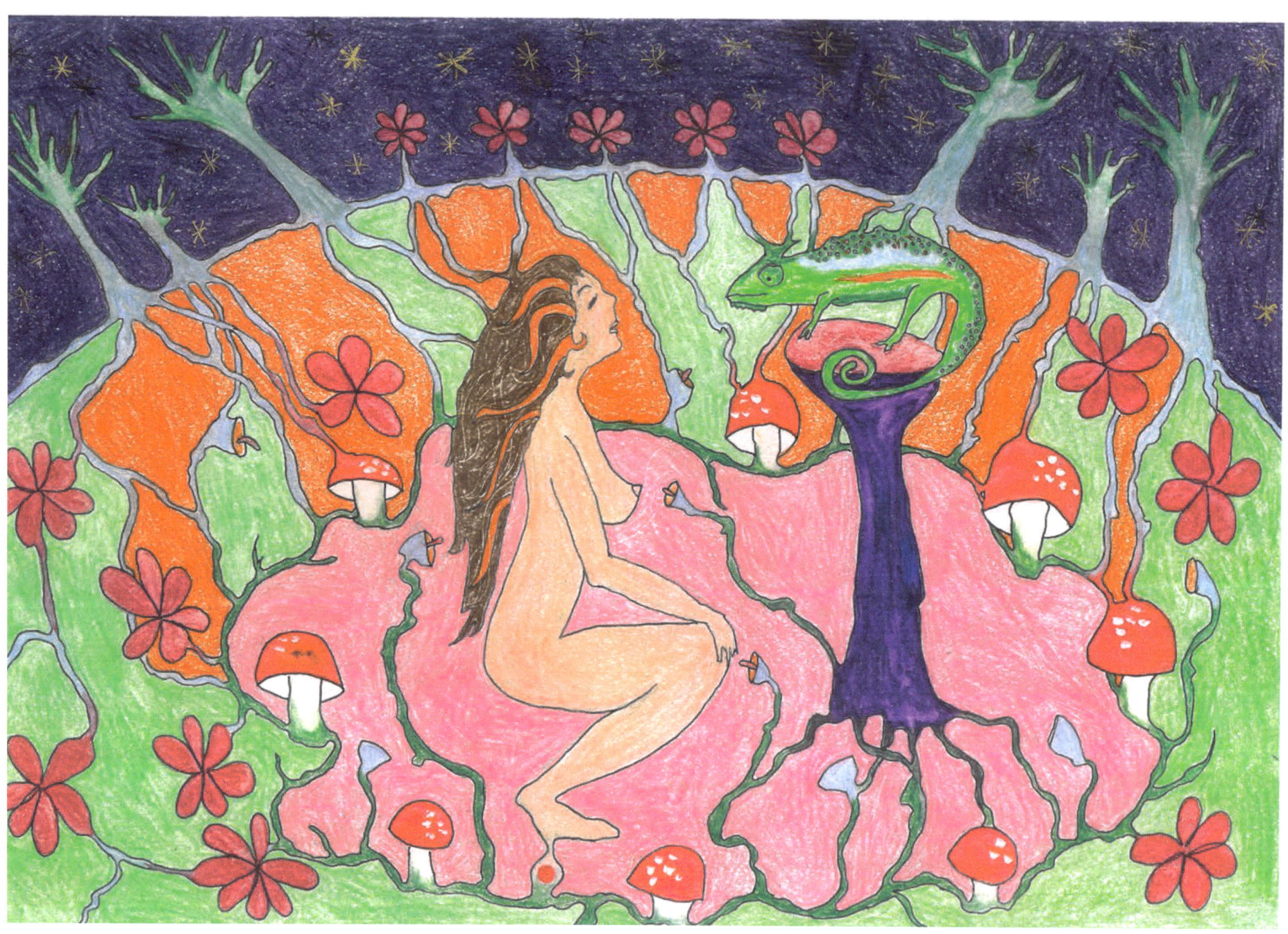

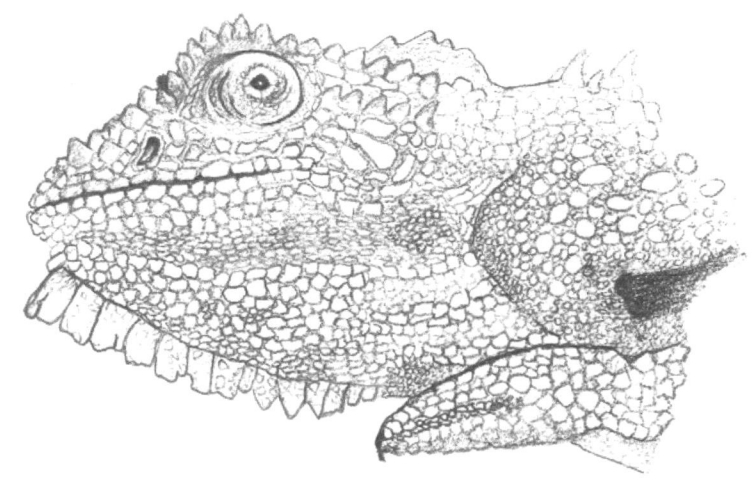

2
UNINTENTIONAL HAPPENINGS

I made many unusual friends. Why? It's my son's fault. Yip, he did it!

My son was always in a pre-school, as I always worked full hours. Some of them he liked, some of them he didn't. I later found out that most of his real, early preschool days were spent with the gardener outside, as he was plain difficult indoors, and so as a rescue plan, the teacher sent him outside to be in his happy place. Once again, I never knew this.

Anyhow, when real school started, I enrolled him in a standard school, which was just a disaster. My child had been running around in a superhero outfit for 6 years, and now he had to wrestle on a uniform and sit and draw.

Yes, sit and draw. His favourite superhero was batman. He had all the suits. If Batman was not available, he would switch to Spiderman and his least favourite... Superman.

One night with family visiting we found Roger in the bath, fully clothed in his Batman suit. He was taking his bath. He ran around barefoot and clothed in grey. He was as wild as his mother. He was not a child who wanted stuff... but he did want "man" toys... like a pellet gun and a motorbike.

I could not say no. So, at 7 years old he was hunting guinea fowl and riding a 100CC motorbike. Too short, he would have to either do a kinda running start or climb a rock to mount the bike. His maermerrics[6] were purple and blue, but he taught himself.

So, back to his first year in school... My child, I could see, was unhappy, and it did look like a depression was settling in. I was called in for the standing and drawing and he had problems focusing. Of course it did not help that I saw nothing wrong in Roger choosing to stand while drawing.

One year he endured. I went to all the parent/teacher meetings blah blah blah – and had to hear that my child must go to a "special" class. You know the story. It of course did not sit right with me.

My goodness! There was nothing wrong with my child's intelligence. I went to the first meeting in the next grade, and had to look at an empty classroom, devoid of any colour, but a huge poster declaring what was not allowed. Now I was brisling. I took him out the next day without a plan. I had to find a school. An unusual school.

I found the Waldorf School not far from our little farm. You see that.... our farm. By now I had established a proprietary (... ness) in my mind. I was farming. Amongst other things, of course.

I went to a meeting, and they were still saying something about meeting Roger, and deciding on if he was suited.... all very fuzzy in my mind, and that blah blah blah thing was happening again, and at the end I basically just told the teachers that they have no choice. Roger has to go to school at the Waldorf School.

I would not accept a no. A school with a unique philosophy (wacky, some would say... our saving grace in my opinion). The children wore no uniforms, no emblems, cell phones were not allowed. They could have their hair long, boys and girls alike. It was a school made for my son and I. We loved it.

Being focused on an organic lifestyle and the teachings of Rudolf Steiner, the school did attract some unusual characters. We all shared a passion for healthy food, and most of my new girlfriends were interested in organic gardening. We all felt like we found our tribe.

We shared many philosophies, which extended to helping each other raise our kids. It was a wonderful place to be. Our friendships remain until today.

DA CASE OF DA HUNGRY PIGS

Roger was about 15. Delicate age. I lost my job. No income. My brother was trying to help us financially while my friend and I got a sassy sauce company off the ground. Maiden's Tongue, a chili sauce-inspired company, saw the light of day. We worked hard, but my feed bill was huge. Three Great Danes, 4 other types of dogs, 11 pigs, chickens, a cat, a diabetic son with a special diet... ooooh, it was not easy.

Just outside of the school, a company was packaging salads and vegetables for a green grocery chain with very strict hygiene and quality requirements. Huge dumpsters were placed at the back. Beautiful produce was discarded as it did not meet the chain's standards. Well now, what luck.

My Portuguese friend Lucia, short as her fuse, strongly built, black ponytail, also a farmer, ever practical and solid.... We climbed into the dumpsters and helped ourselves. Fresh produce and lo and behold, a perfect cauliflower... and perfect corn. To be honest.... we do suspect a bit of skulduggery was probably afoot. But only later.

At that stage we just saw fresh food.

So, every day after school, we would stop at the dumpsters. Our kids were expected to help, and to give them a lot of credit, they climbed in with us and helped us gather food for our menagerie. These kids knew the situation. They knew what had to be done. In full view of all the parents and kids going home... that took courage...and maturity!

DA CASE OF DA BIG EMBARRASSMENT

Roger had never been embarrassed by his mother. True. He was always proud of my accomplishments and our humble life on the farm. He valued his freedom and saw in his mother a person that saw in him. He always could speak his mind. I would always listen. Differences in opinions were welcomed. I never had a rude child... ok only once, and I will tell the story still, maybe.

His class were forging steel and carving wood, and I always helped with the unusual requests. Their next project was leather tanning, and in true Waldorf style, it had to be done as the Stone Age people would do it. It did entail the brains of an animal...

Here comes Super Mother. Super excited to learn all I could about traditional tanning methods. I knew a couple who had a goat farm, and the young males were a problem. As a means to make some cash, I sold young, slaughtered goats to a few restaurants.
At the appointed time, mom arrives at the school not only with 10 skins, but 10 goat heads. Now goats have really strange eyes, and a body-less goat (in hindsight) is probably not something you should show 15 young adults, half of them vegetarian and the other half oblivious of the origin of the skinless chicken breast they have for supper.

One girl lost her lunch, quite a few fainted and my son stared at me in the same manner as the bodiless goats were staring at us.

We revived the ones who fainted and cleaned up the lunch-less girl. There was a bit of mayhem. Wonder upon wonder, I received an invitation for the lesson in tanning. How the teacher got most to participate, he would only know.

Well, tanning is a tough business, and using the brains of goats has certain drawbacks. I don't know if it was supposed to smell like it did... some fainted again and someone else lost their lunch. A few pressed forwards.

My fingers fell off. I found them. They fell off again. I think I found them... I ended up with a stiff board. You could surf on it. If it smelt better, you could serve a roast on it. I took my pathetic attempts home and threw it on the chicken cage roof. A wind took them and deposited the skins in our garden.

The dogs found them and used them as giant chews. My son stared at me like a bodiless goat. He was not impressed. We never spoke of that again, until much later when as an adult, I asked him whether I had ever embarrassed him. He looked at me, I saw a goat, and I knew.

GARDEN STORIES

My hands were always in the soil. Childhood memories became adult realities and, true to my path, I stumbled upon composting.

Google was a fart in the universe. I knew nothing of composting, which is very apparent in my early writings. This attitude of actually knowing less than fuckall about something, and subsequently winging it all the way, runs through my life like the blood running through my veins.

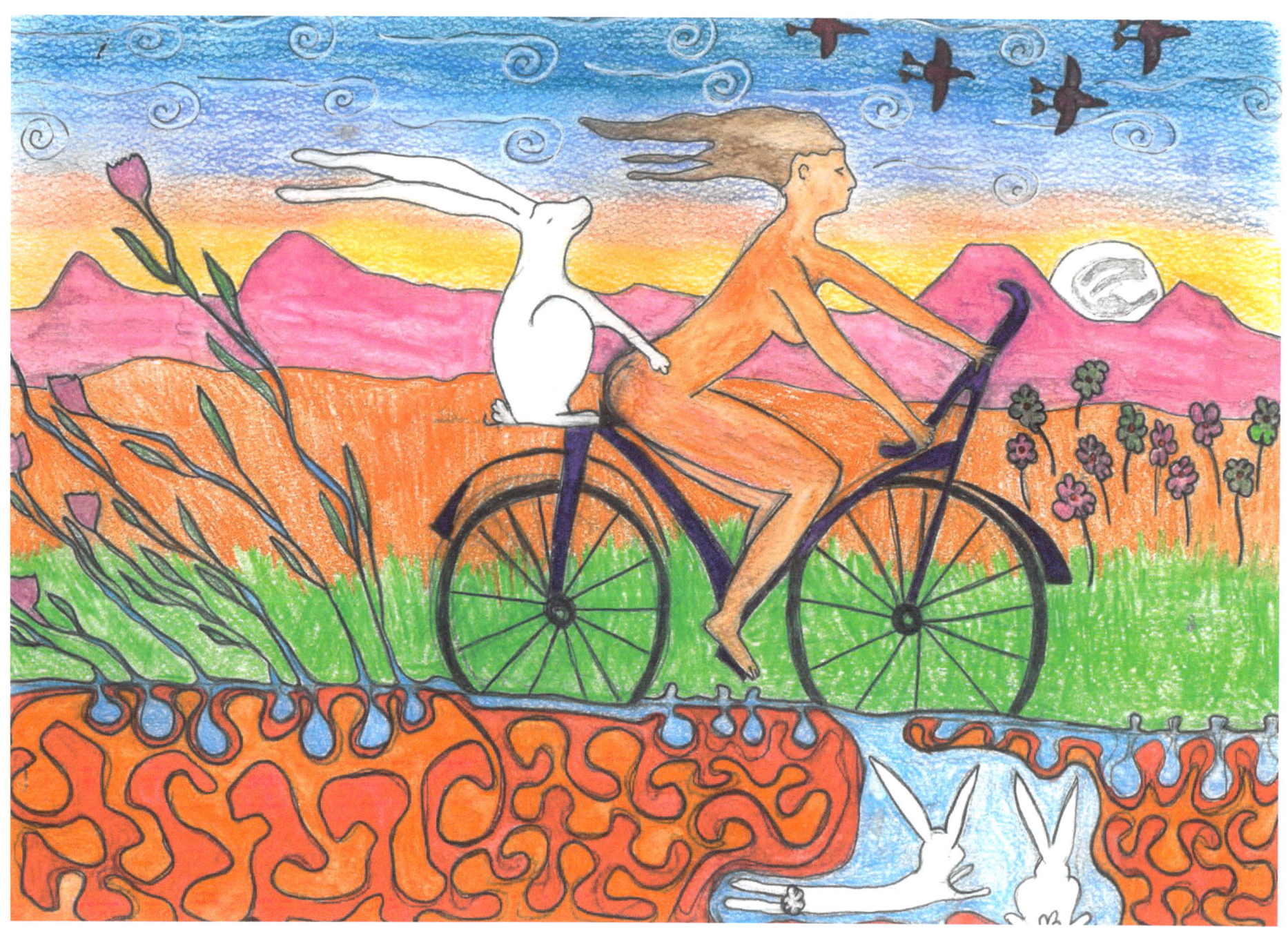

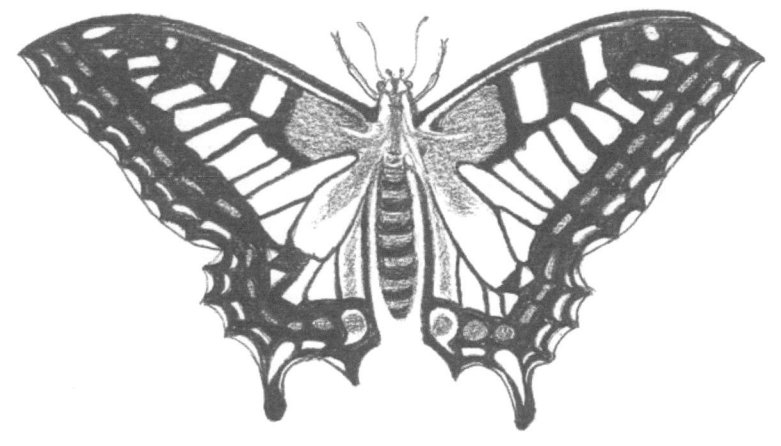

3
MY WINGING ATTITUDE

My earliest memory of this was as a child teaching all the kids in the school to do Spanish dancing. We had a wooden stage which, when not in use, was piled up under a canopy. So up on high, here I am, teaching everyone to do Spanish dancing, while I myself was only learning.

Another memory was with our matric farewell, which I organised with great gusto. Not only did I paint humongous murals, but also took on the role as flower arranger. Both my efforts looked hideous, but in my eyes they were masterpieces.

Where I got this can-do attitude can only be attributed to my bloodline, which was hectically mixed with the original Dutch settlers, and some German blood intermingled with a good dash of English.

My forefathers sailed from their homeland just because they were fed up for several reasons (some religious, I believe), and came to the southernmost tip of Africa, where they found the Bushmen and San people.

At one stage they got fed up with the lot in the Cape, and took their ox wagons, animals, children and wives and did another we-are-fucking-off-cause-we-don't-like-who's-in-charge. Apparently also religiously inspired.

They trekked over ridiculously perilous terrain; the hardships of those hardy souls are well-documented in our history. We developed our own language. Who does that? We took on the mighty England. Who does that when you are a few thousand strong? So I suppose my whole life is a testament to my bloodline.

I was working as a prosecutor at the law courts in Port Elizabeth, and married Rogers' dad. For no other reason than to go and see how other people lived, we moved to America, with the idea of spending 18 months there, but ended up staying for 8 years. Roger was born, and I decided to return to Africa, minus the husband, and our life started again in Africa.

A friend (who had many animals) offered us a gorgeous black potbelly pig, whom we named Sonneblom[7]. She was best friends with Didi, our young mongrel pup. I put a nappy on her, and she lived with us until she became a little bit too big for our tiny cottage, and their plays became a little too serious. A bite from a pig can break a dog's paw. So that resulted in some camps being built in a hurry (and once again winging it)... they were at best 50% effective to keep Sonneblom in.

Sustainability was always part of my life. The desire to know where your meat came from, how the animals were kept, how the slaughter process was executed. To grow your own vegetables, collect your own eggs... this became a passion and with the passing years, a big reality. Not that I knew what it entailed to keep pigs, and how to slaughter them. No... that I would learn in time. I was so ignorant. My idea was to slaughter the children of Sonneblom.

Now this might seem cruel, and it probably is. So Mielie[8] came to the farm. His great grandfather was a wild bush pig, and so Mielie looked wild. He had huge shoulders that tapered down to very slim hips. An absolute specimen of a pig, with big wild-looking tusks.

He was, however, the gentlest of creatures. He fathered many, whom we duly slaughtered. Sonneblom would absolutely do her nut, running up and down the fence, and for a month I could not dare enter her pen as she was likely to bite me.

The intelligence of pigs is what I learnt through that whole experience. They are delightful and clean, contrary to what the popular belief is, but yes, they do enjoy a mud bath (but that does not make them dirty). They will never roll in their own faeces, unless confined in such small surroundings that they have no other choice.

Two pigs became 11 pigs, and keeping them fenced was another story. Countless times Roger and I would be chasing them through the vineyards next to the small cottage we rented, as pigs running amok amongst precious vineyards would not be appreciated. It was hilarious. Me screaming at the top of my lungs that the whole valley could hear...

WHEN IS 'WINGING IT' THE SAME AS BULLSHITTING?

My brother Wynand and I became very fond of mushroom foraging. We were hypercautious and conservative, as my brother explained in great detail the death that awaits careless foragers, and I was not ready for my liver to turn into jelly (literally emulsify!), as I was planning on curing it until the Grim Reaper comes and points his ugly finger at me. Hey, you there! Enough is enough.

It is a fun pursuit, but the dangers are real. So over time we have learnt to pick about 7 different species. On one such foraging expedition we came upon the motherload. Ahead in a clearing, porcini, the king of all mushrooms, were spread, beautiful, we were ecstatic. We could not contain ourselves, and took them all.

Our plan was to dry them as there was just too much. We had been a bit careless, and so sat with many that were covered in sand. I winged it and said we should wash them, and then put them in the drier. My

brother was a bit unsure, but I said it with such confidence...
Next morning an irate, furious brother was on the line kakking[9] me out from a dizzy height. They had all turned into a stinking, jellied fuck-up. He was beside himself.

What a waste and it was a huge mess. My winging it was actually bullshitting.

THE STORY OF THE BIG PIG THAT WAS SMALL

It was decided for me to spitbraai[10] one of the big pigs. Sam, my male Great Dane had bitten one of the adult pigs for the second time and my birthday was coming up so fuck it, lets spit the pig. I am not going to the vet for the second time with the same pig with the same wound. The pigs I kept were not meat pigs, they were a mixture of wild boar and Transkei pigs, who were mostly kept for making soap as their meat and fat ratio were suited to that operation.

Well, here I am, winging it again... I invited a whole bunch of people and set about spitting a specimen of my big pigs. The spitting went on and on... on and on... the pig got smaller and smaller. After a while it was not even necessary to add any charcoal.

The fat dripping was enough to keep things going. Truth be told I had to dampen quite a few flames down. The pig got smaller and smaller. My guests were truly, desperately hungry. They were all truly drunk, the pig looked like a small dog, and all went home hungry.

SLIP SLIDING AWAY

I tried my hand at everything. One of my projects was broilers. How difficult can that be? I built a cage and bought 500 chicks. Who does that? 500 chicks that become 500 fat broilers. 500 broilers that have to be slaughtered at some or other stage. The 500 chicks outgrew their cage, and I was forced to free-range them on the back stoep[11]. Not thinking of the horrendous stench and mess that would occur right on my doorstep, I let them free. 500 big fat broilers... all they do is eat and crap. It was a nightmare. I called my friends to help slaughter.

If memory serves me well, we were about 5 friends slaughtering 500 broilers. We were slip-sliding all over the place, catching and slaughtering. And now where do you put 500 broilers? I did have a few freezers but 500... am I crazy! My friends who helped got their fair share. But this whole episode while I was working full time. What the hell?

Elize offered to continue on the Monday, and I have a distinct memory of finding my bath full of slaughtered chickens. Bless her soul, she had nowhere to put them, so the bath was the best option. Somehow I got them in the freezers, and we had chicken for months. Years.

Here is a funny fact about broilers. They certainly are stupid. Their DNA is to eat and eat and eat. And crap. That they do in abundance. So you start slaughtering, and none of them know the difference. If you have 50 and you have slaughtered about 45 of them, the ones left are starting to notice something. Not sure what, but something is happening... By the time you get to broiler number 48, it has dawned on him that they are getting less, and it could only mean one thing. So those last 2 are the clever ones. and catching them is kak[12] difficult ....

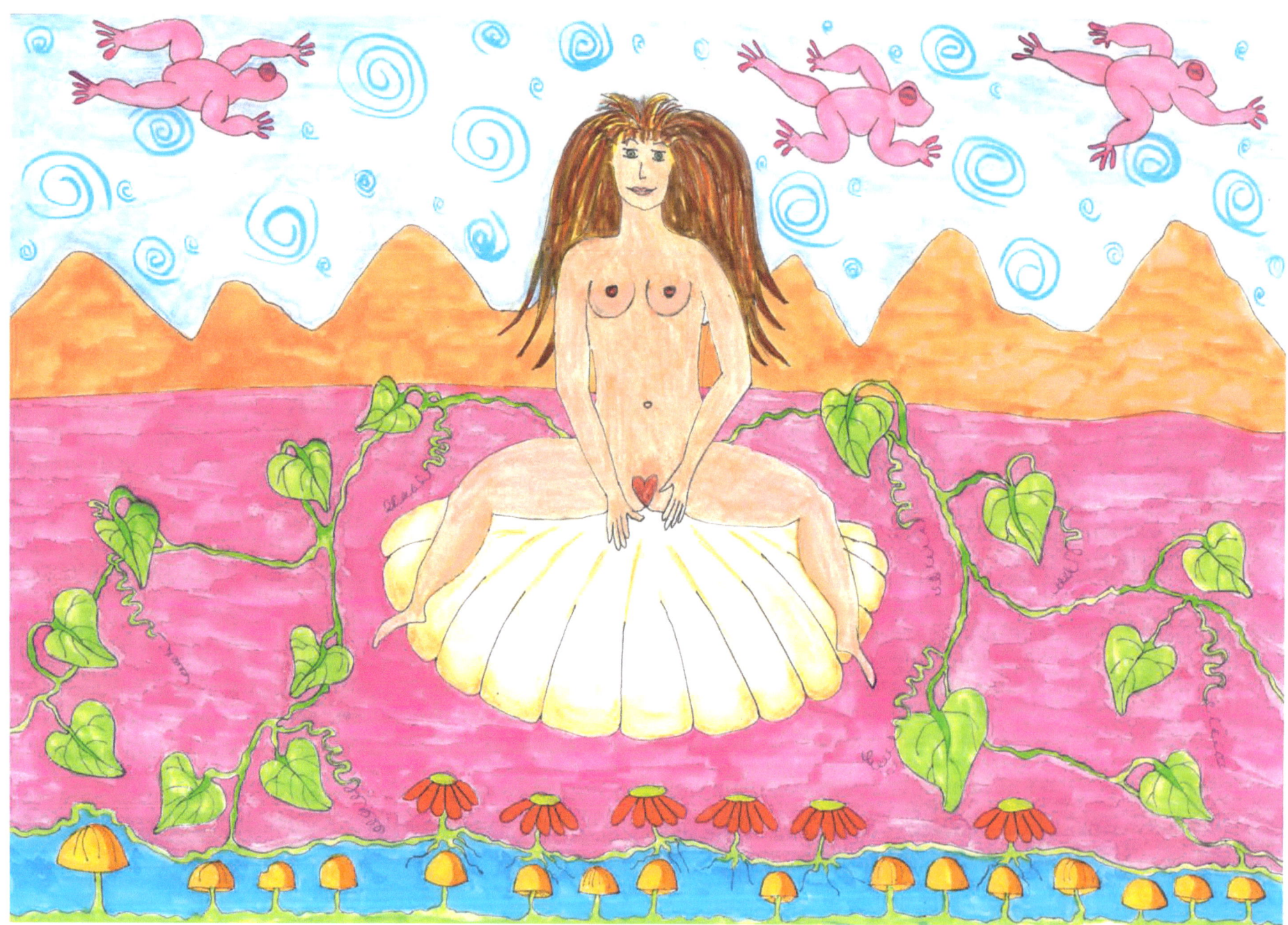

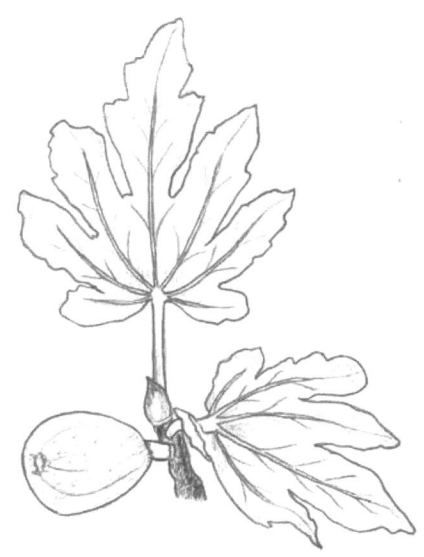

4
HARVEST TIME

My favourite part of harvesting was creating recipes from scratch. My creations were often very elaborate, which I could never remember. Friends would feast on our harvest, and years later would remind me of this-and-that dish that they could just not forget, but it was lost in my mind of future dishes. Depending on what was ready to harvest, I would invent a recipe.

OF PUMPKINS, MAGIC AND BLACK GOLD
BOLANDER, APRIL 15 2009

There is nothing as beautiful, so alluring, as a steaming heap of compost. This year I have earnestly attempted the creation of the biggest compost heap in the history of gardening.

It has taken every scrap of organic material my garden has to offer: I have bravely included all the weeds, as I am confident my heap will reach the magical temperature of, I believe, 65 to 70 degrees Celsius. Editor's Note: I must have discovered Google.

I have to confess that I am more or less the bull-in-a-china-shop type of gardener. – Editor's Note: If ever a truth was spoken. I go where most gardeners fear to tread. It is mostly a hit-and-miss business, but so far the gardening angels have looked after me with mostly hits.

Anyway, I'm digressing. Compost heaps, compost heaps!

So, I have added a few bags of Willem's exotic manure. I covered my mountain with an old tent, compliments of my Great Danes (who decided it was a great toy and tore a huge hole in one side) That leaves me with something resembling a new informal settlement, and I am fervently hoping that things are heating up and the earthworms are happy and doing what earthworms do best.- Editor's Note. Earthworms will start populating the compost heap when temperatures go down. This summer I harvested the most beautiful white pumpkins, or as we say, boerpampoene[13] .

STUFFED BOERPAMPOEN

INGREDIENTS:

1 handsome boerpampoen (size does matter – not too big as it gets heavy)
2 to 3 cups of cooked brown rice, once again depending on size
About 4 sage leaves
4 cloves of garlic
2 onions
2 cups of finely chopped fresh parsley
A handful of roasted nuts, any variety
Dried apricots (chopped and/or raisins)
A punnet of mushrooms
Feta to taste, cubed
Cubed butter, if desired
Salt and ground black pepper to taste
10 pork sausages, removed from casings

METHOD:

Cut a lid out of the pumpkin and remove all the seeds.
Sauté chopped onion, mushroom, garlic and add chopped nuts to roast. Remove from heat and add to brown rice.

Fill the pumpkin with mixture and close the lid. Wrap in tin foil and pop in the oven at 180°C for one hour. This tin foiled treasure can also be cooked on a fire, but then you must know what you are doing. Take that baby out of the oven and transfer it to the table with extremely dramatic gestures.

You will experience audible breaths being sucked in and a reverent silence will descend. Guaranteed!

It is fool proof, impressive and wonderfully aromatic and incredibly healthy. Well, leave the butter and sausage out if you want it that healthy. Editor's Note: No, don't do that. It's what makes this recipe great.

Using sage in this recipe reminds me of a conundrum I have had since I have started my vegetable garden. I am convinced that sage does not like me. It's unfair, I love sage, especially fried in butter and strewn over pasta.

It refuses to return my love. I have planted it in perfect conditions, watered it judiciously, but no! It conspires behind my back, it forms suicide pacts and dies.

So on this depressing note I will leave you with the following: If you have any comments or questions, email Bolander and I will do my best to respond to whatever is required.

If it falls outside my practical experience I will find the correct solutions. I know just enough to be dangerous, but don't worry – nothing has exploded in my garden, yet.

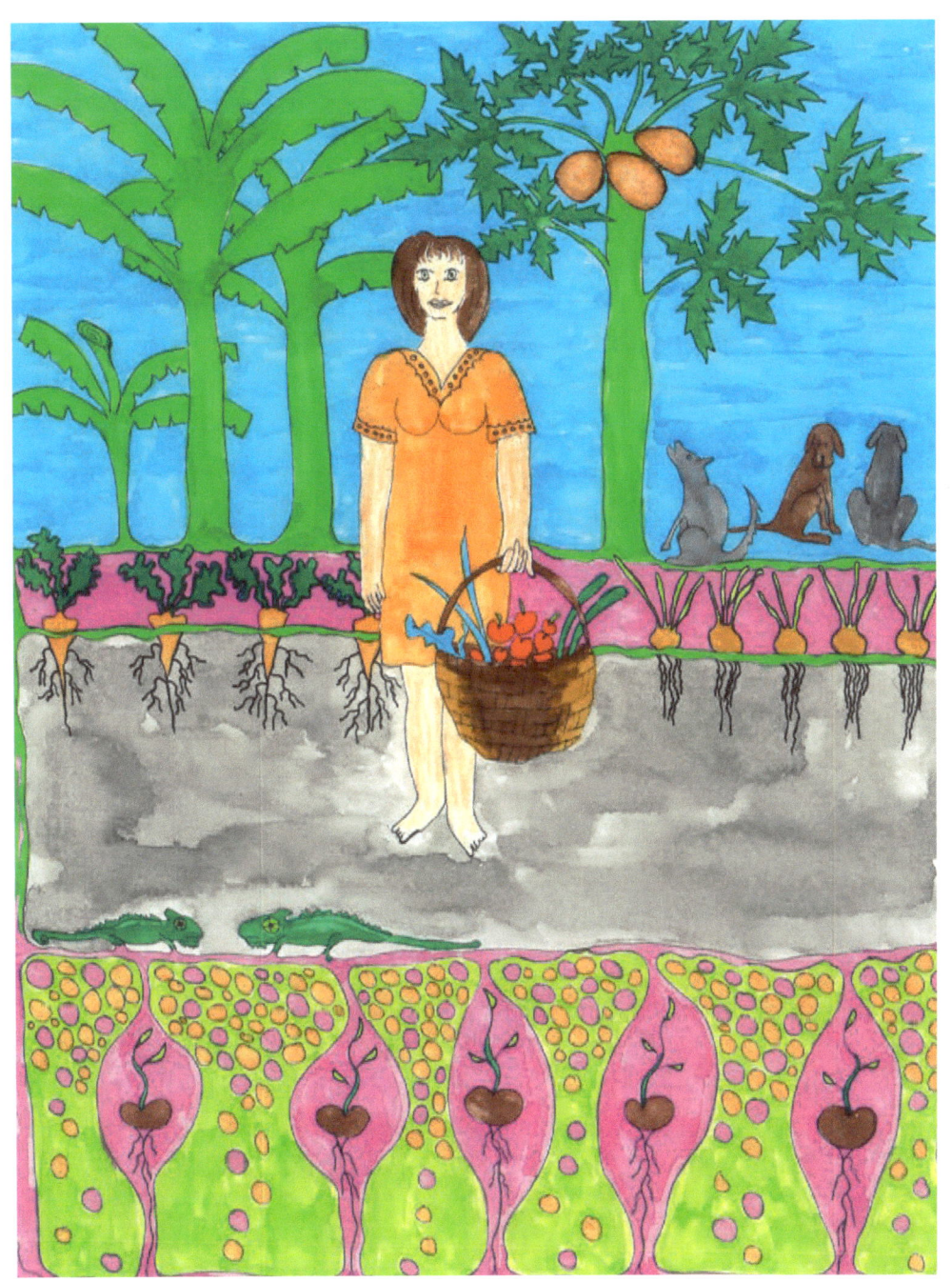

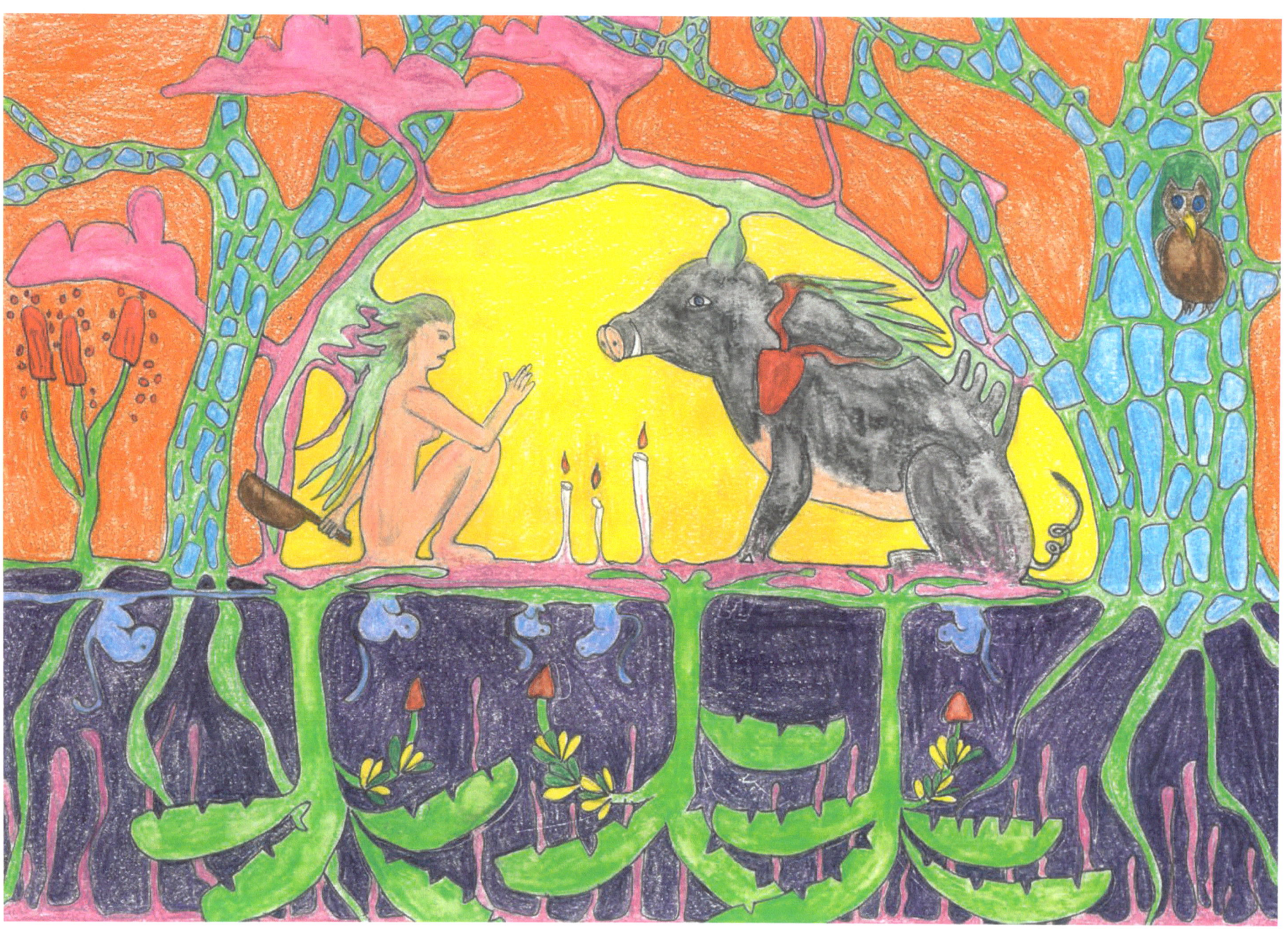

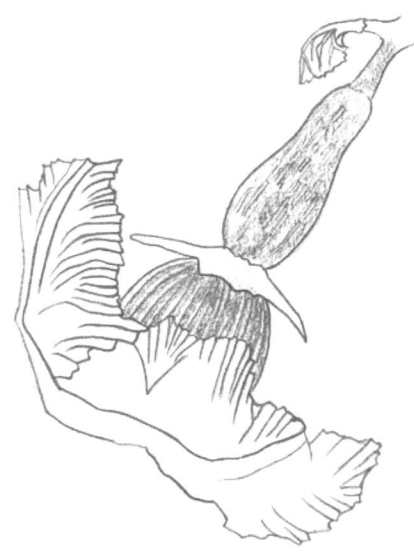

5
TRADITIONS

There was always an abundance of some or other crop. Whether it was green figs to then make the yummiest green fig preserve, or peaches to make a sweet curry pickle (which Selma and I blessed with the name Peach Mischief) or tomatoes for days, to make a beautiful fragrant marinara sauce, I needed friends to help. So the tradition of assisting was born.

Whomever was available would come and join the peeling and cutting up of the harvest. As a means of reward for all the hard work, I would barter the product for their labour of love. Ample wine had to be consumed and it always ended up in a raucous party and a whole day affair. We laughed and cried and hashed out problems. It was such a blessing to have my girlfriends join in this ancient art of preserving, and until today remains the highlight of the harvesting calendar.

Everyone leaves tired, but in a bliss of love and mutual understanding.

These ties that bind us together as travellers on this path called life.

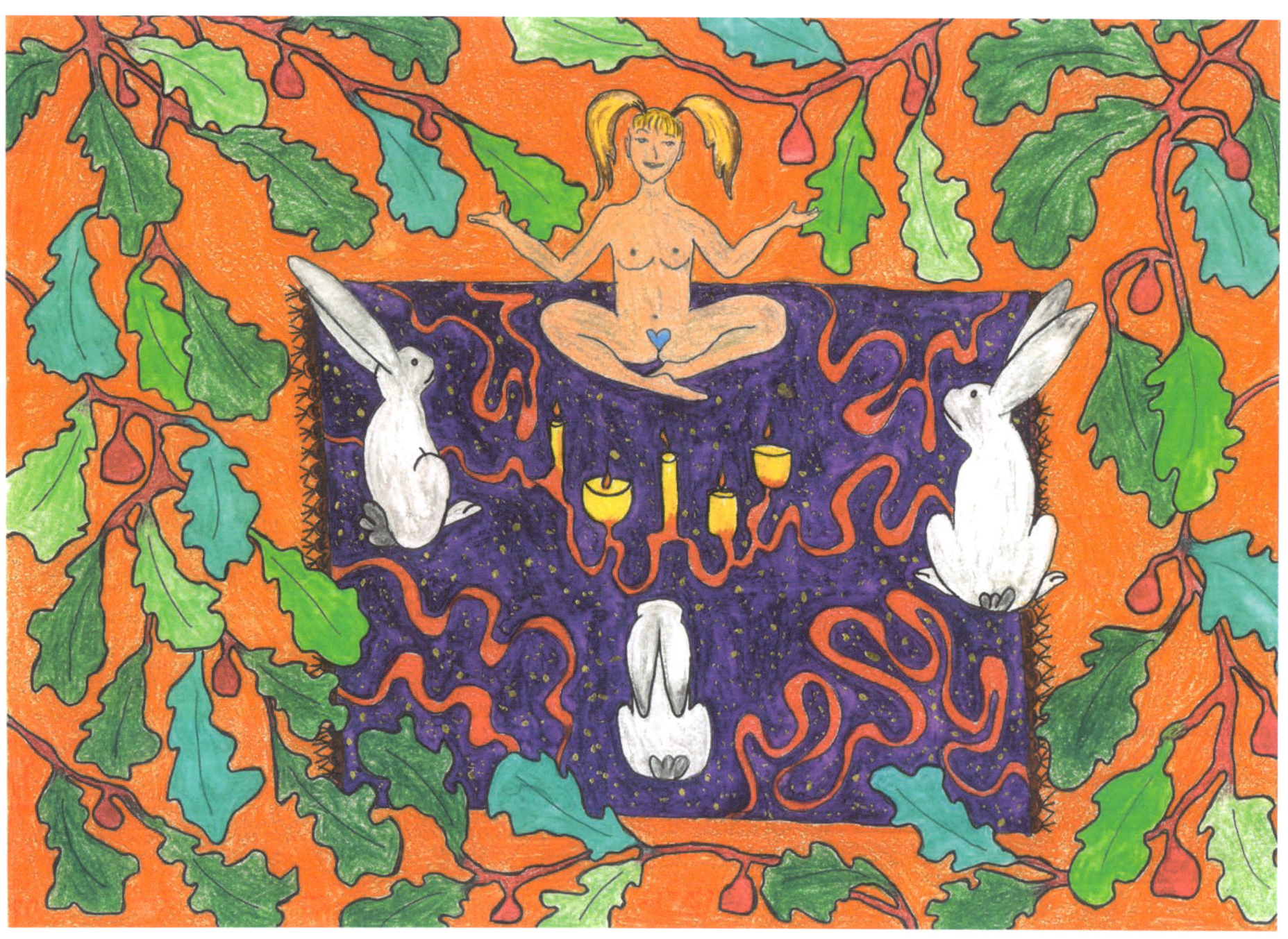

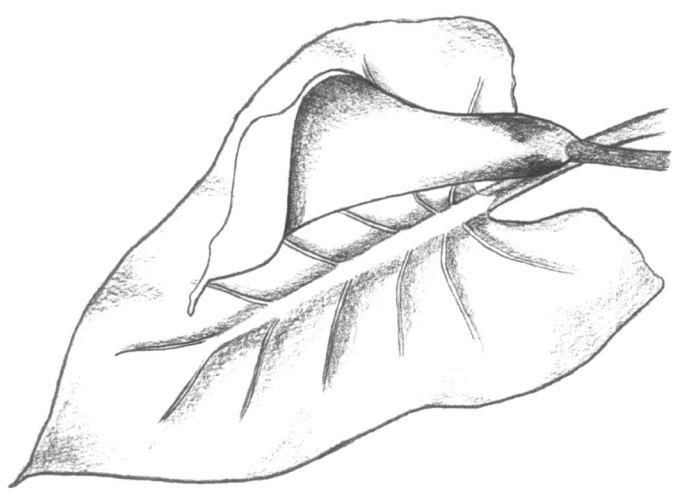

6

FORAGING

Part of a sustainable life is an ability to forage, and mushroom hunting is an activity we look forward to each autumn. We have many forests around our area, and so successfully, without poisoning anyone, have learnt to pick porcini, chicken of the woods, pine rings and a few less favourite boletus species.

South Africa is blessed with many indigenous fruits and plants, and the collection of waterblommetjies[14], a type of water plant reminiscent of green beans, was and remains a favourite pastime during spring. These were jovially shared with friends, and Carolyn, editor of Bolander, wrote a beautiful piece on just one such day.

WATERBLOMMETJIES IN DIE BOLAND
BOLANDER, 7 OCTOBER 2009

Gathered in a rambling garden, with a ceramic baboon staring pensively into the distant mountains, we savored the flavors of the Boland over the weekend.

Our genial host, Anita, had waded into the nearby dam earlier with some friends, to harvest this quintessential crop from the waters, emerging with baskets laden with the succulent plants and their characteristic little white flowers.

Later, the cast-iron potjie[15] simmered away gently on the fire, and in the chameleon-filled garden we sat in quiet communion listening to bird calls as the sun set – transforming the face of the Helderberg[16]

and Stellenbosch Mountains into gorgeous shades of auburn.
Leaning against a (barely bearing) skinny pawpaw tree, propped up against a bamboo ladder on the side of her cottage, reclined a large painting she'd just completed – the serene gaze of a woman in the foreground, winding road receding, mysterious bird in the corner.
In the twilight we all mused on it for a while, and then the smell from the potjie lured us to the candle-laden old table, and we looked over the valley of vines as we ate.

There was a sense of harmony, of melody through elemental communion, encapsulated by this benevolent southern stretch of the African continent. It is October, and the rains of winter are behind us, and the shimmering heat of summer is practically upon us.

Amid the stress and busy pace of life, it is essential to pause, reflect, and express appreciation through moments like these.

There are harvests that surround us at any given moment, and it is up to us to reach out and sample them – a glorious sunset revealing the contours and undulations of the mountains: a long-tailed mouse-bird flitting amongst an aloe's blossoms, the transformation from blank canvas to rendered scene, with brushstroke of paints. Salad from the garden.

Lingering in the moment, sampling heaven on your tongue, through your senses.

Carolyn Frost – Editor

I think she writes much better than I do. Mmmmh. Anyhow, let's talk about the weather.

A TALE OF TALL TREES

Our cottage was so small, and with the years I planted trees that became big trees, and so this is a tale of trees. We faced many storms with winds blowing in excess of 120km/hr.

The old people knew a lot of stuff. A row of huge blue gums ended our property, running up a hill, about 20 strong. They must have been over 100 years old. Majestic. The adjacent farm was bought by foreigners who knew nothing of the mini-climate around our precious little house, and so decided in all their wisdom to cut down all those beautiful trees.

The reason for this will escape me forever and no explanation is going to make sense. I was so freakin' furious. After this sacrilege, a storm of note set in. Next morning I found half our roof on the front lawn. The old people knew stuff. That was a very necessary windbreak. Our little cottage was left exposed, like a mole without sunblock. I wrote about the next storm that ravaged our little paradise.

WATERBLOMMETJIE HARVEST TIME
BOLANDER, 11 NOVEMBER 2009

Nature has a funny way of showing you who is boss. Once again, I had to play second fiddle to the howling wind, helplessly inadequate to aid my fig tree – who was succumbing tragically to Mother Nature. Cruel she can be, aye.

Whilst this little drama was taking place, my nameless tree (and this is another long story best left for another day) was precariously heaving over, roots uplifted, ready to snap.

As I fear nothing, I sent my son up on the roof with a saw, wind blowing at hurricane speed, with anguished instructions to lob off half the tree. Being the fruit of my loins (why can only men say that, it sounds so good?), he jumped eagerly to task and saved the day like Mr. Muscle (only it was not a stove he had to save).

The upside to all this mayhem was that I had green figs, and I eagerly set forth to make green fig preserve, which did come out so fantastically – and if anyone wants a foolproof recipe on green fig preserve, let me know. I just don't know how you will time it with a howling wind and a succumbed fig tree. Oh, I'm just pulling your leg. Meanwhile, a week prior to this huge storm, we were peacefully harvesting waterblommetjies from a dam close to my cottage. I cannot emphasize enough what a privilege it is to pick your own waterblommetjies.

And because I have access to an abundance of these delicate, beautiful plants, I choose only the flowers. Yeah I know, I'm spoiled!

A GREAT UNTRADITIONAL WAY TO COOK WATERBLOMMETJIES IS AS FOLLOWS:

Boil three medium sized potatoes with skin until just before ready (ok, so if you boil them past this delicate point it will not be a train smash).

Chop 4 to 5 really big onions with green leaves, if you have them in the garden that I told you to start (don't worry, I know this sounds and looks like a whole lotta onions, but just trust me)

4 garlic cloves, chopped

Well washed young waterblommetjies (wash in salted water), about a heaped ice cream container full

Salt and pepper to taste

About a quarter cup of extra virgin olive oil and two generous tablespoons of butter (if you are health conscious leave out the butter, but you know I won't recommend it)

Use a wok and skin the potatoes and roughly cut up in blocks. Finely chop up all the onions plus green leaves, or substitute with chives or spring onions leaves. Add garlic and waterblommetjies. Add butter and olive oil.

Now put all of this on a humongously hot fire, whether it be coals or gas is om't ewe [17]. Cook until waterblommetjies are al dente. Add salt and pepper to taste. This is divine.

So... food, the collecting of food (and the subsequent cooking of it) played a big part in our lives. I never forced Roger to work in the garden; I always thought that it would be unfair to expect the same passion from someone else. He grew up with an abundance of organic produce. Healthy, delicious.

Mealtimes were occasions. The most difficult aspect of it was that I worked full day, picked him up at aftercare, and as soon as we entered the house I would hear these dreaded words... Ma I'm hungry. And boy, was he hungry. So often meals were quick and wholesome. I became an expert in snappy cuisine. Roger became diabetic at the age of 13, so to adjust to his requirements, I had to

31

get quite imaginative with food, as pastas, bread, pizzas and fast food were out of the window.

Now I can hear you saying pizza is not fast food... not the way I made it. Yes, we never bought any fast food, as we lived very far from any shops, and deliveries did not extend to our little cottage. So until today, I do not know what it is like to open my door and a man with a pizza box appears. Things other people take for granted, and here it just is not part of our reality.

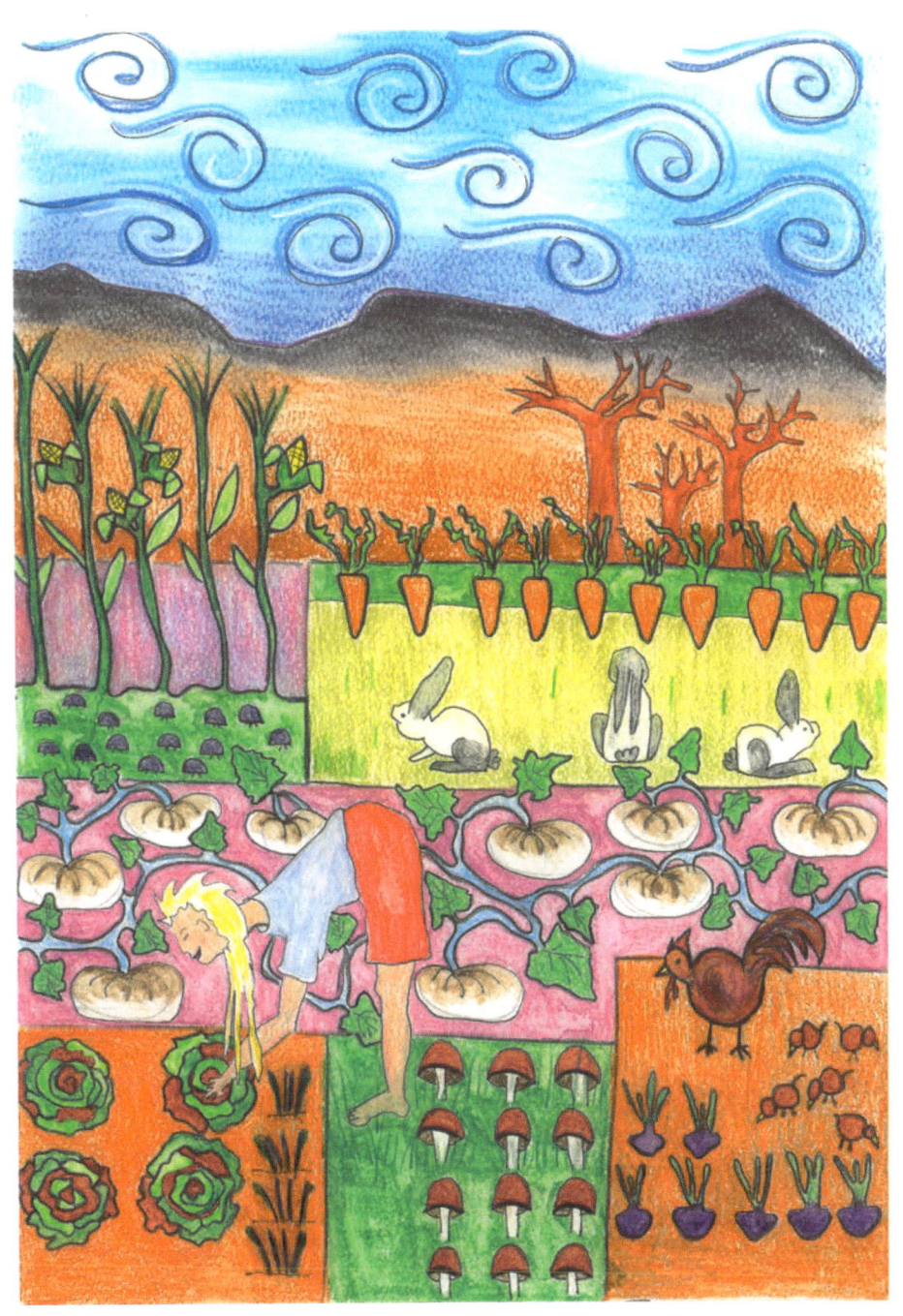

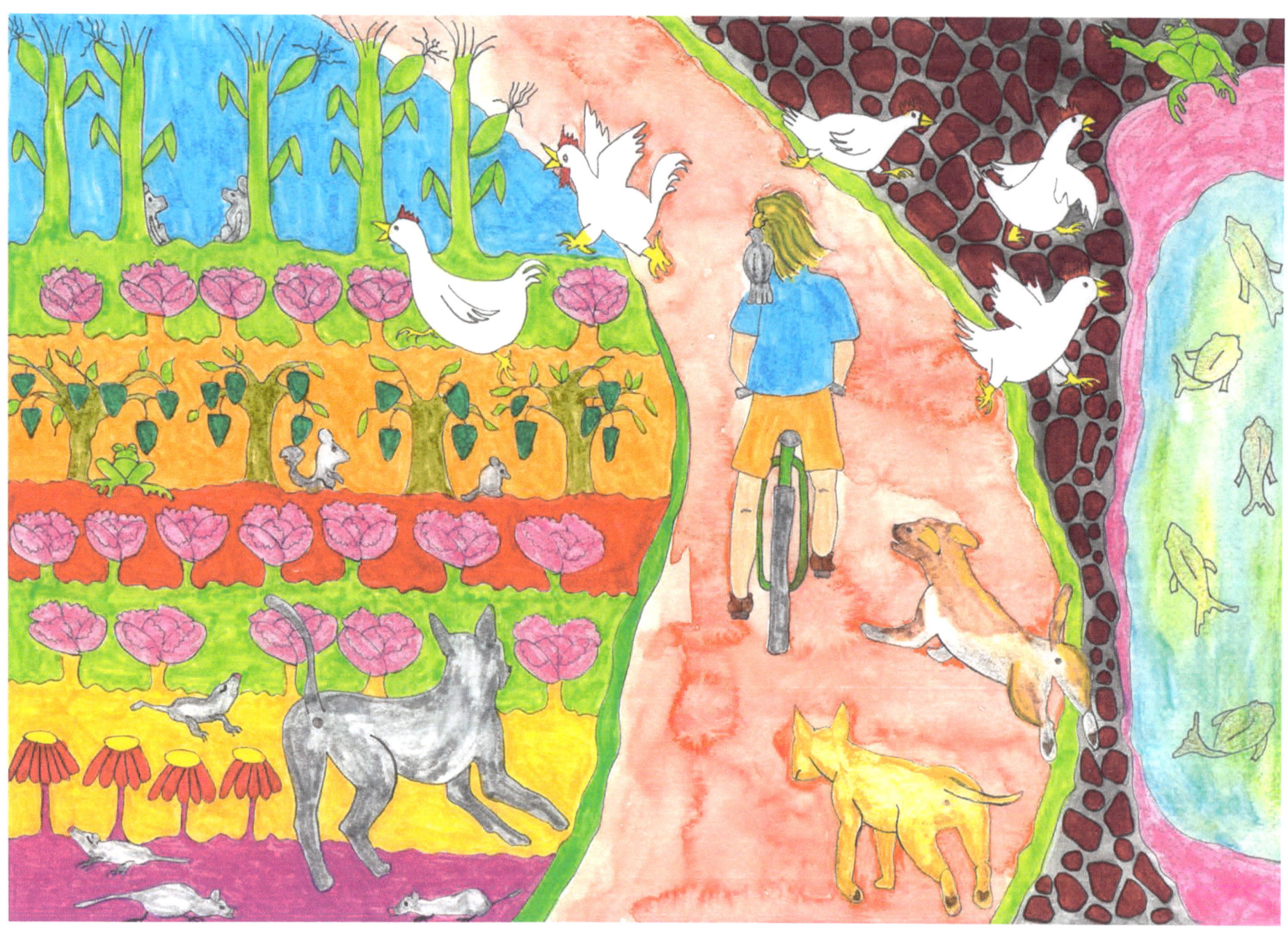

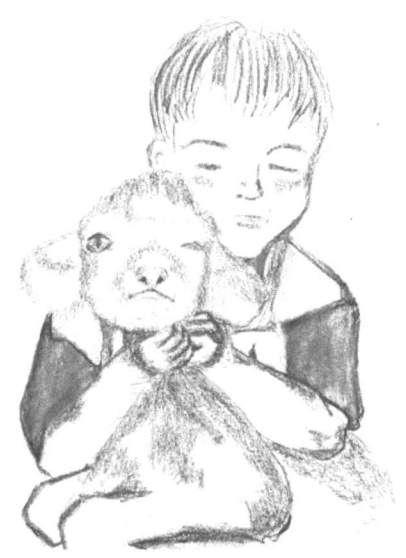

7

ROGER

My son and I lived in our cottage without many interruptions, the biggest one being a very ill-thought -out instant marriage when he was about 10, which did not last more than a year. I do not dwell much on mistakes, and don't see my choices as bad or wrong... but that choice... oh, that was not a good one.

So I was never one to have long-lasting relationships, mostly saw casual relationships whenever it felt right which was when my son was with his dad. Yes, probably a double life, but I did not see the point in involving my son in my tumultuous love life. I gave my love freely and kissed a whole bunch of frogs on the way that were not polite enough to change into princes.

Roger inherited my love of animals, and he had quite the selection (the sequence of when he kept what is a bit fuzzy).

I remember keeping a lamb when we just moved into the cottage, as our neighbour's sheep had twins and he did not think that the mother could look after both. Roger had just turned two. We raised him successfully into sheephood when he started bumping stuff. I sent him off to another farm instead of slaughtering him... what was I thinking... and subsequently he was bitten by one of their dogs and had to be slaughtered.

Roger was about 4 when I bought him his first cockatiel. Grey with yellow fluffs around his cheeks. The bird went everywhere with Roger. Sat on his shoulder clinging for dear life as Roger went flying

35

down the hill on his little bike. One day I was busy in the kitchen and saw him run past me with the bird. Just his demeanour... something was wrong.

I went to check on the bird and there he sat, obviously mortally wounded. Much later I got the story out of Roger. They were throwing stones, as all boys do, and one hit his beloved cockatiel. End of the cockatiel. He was distraught. His little face was red and tear-stained. A terrible burden. I got him another cockatiel. I mean how different can they be? He could never bond with him, and the cockatiel became my responsibility.

I could never say no if Roger asked for an animal. I think it was because I was just as excited as he was. Skip a few years and he asked if he could keep a snake. Now I am not a fan of snakes, and we have plenty of cobras on the farm. They are poisonous as hell and I generally try to leave them alone, but when they threaten our dogs and us... head off.

I went to the pet shop and inspected what was available. A beautiful corn snake with black and white piano stripes on his tummy caught my eye. R1500.

That was expensive. Very expensive. I bought it. That was the beginning of many further snakes. The corn snake with its striking orange patterns and perfect piano notes was exotic and beautiful. It escaped many times and we would find it in the garden. No big deal. One day, on exactly such a day where we could not find the damn snake, I found myself on the stoep minding my own business. Around the corner of my house, walk in four gay and proud of it women, Darryll and her friends (she was living in a small cottage on the same farm, about 1km away as the proverbial crow flies).

Now Darryll was an extremely interesting character. She was openly gay and openly free. She walked topless with boobs bouncing up and down. In South Africa amongst the European population, that is just not done. At that stage we were an extremely conservative society. I said hi. They said hi. She asked if they could walk in my garden. Of course.

Next thing here comes the topless Darryll with an exotic orange snake draped around her breasts. She had found Roger's snake.
In order to feed this snake, we had to buy pinkies (small little newborn rats). Roger would feed them to his snake without a qualm. But one day, the snake did not want to eat the pinkie. Roger asked if he could keep the pinkie.

No, I said, no but with a qualification. We would keep the pinkie with the snake overnight. If he survived the snake and he survived the cold (as it was in the middle of the winter), he could keep it and we would call him Hercules.

Well, the next morning the little rat was still there. Stiff as a board. Roger duly picked him up, revived him somehow, and took him to school. Undetected by the teachers, Hercules grew into a huge rat with massive balls. He sat on Rogers shoulder, companion for life. Hercules even went with to PicknPay. Secretly hiding in Rogers' hair and his hoodie. We definitely would have been booted out of that grocery shop if they had known. So he became quite fat and mom decided to put him on the stoep on a very hot day.

No direct sun, but it was a very, very hot day. When we got home, the poor thing had gotten sunstroke and was in his death throes.
We tried to revive him with some cool water but it was too late. I did feel so sad as Hercules was a miracle, and my son bonded with him as no other person could.

We had the corn snake for quite some time and the snake became a specimen. Its demise came when the farm painters washed their brushes under my tap and came upon this bright, expensive snake. Now being very afraid of any snake ordinarily, this bright, exotic snake quadrupled their fear and they unceremoniously chopped its head off with a spade. This R1500 snake that grew into a probably R5000 snake.

By this time we had our own little production line going with a breeding white rat pair. The pinkies would be given to the snake, but what we did not realize was that snakes don't eat that often, and the production line was out of control. We had rats coming out of our ears. It was a real problem.

The pet shops were not interested....what to do what to do? Ok Roger, let's release them at the top dam? We calmed our conscience with the thought that they would return to the wild. Yes, right...

These white rats stuck out like sore thumbs in the brown vegetation. The birds of prey made a killing... so to speak. The damn rats could not blend in. The workers in the vineyards would find one and bring him back! OMW. What the hell. We are trying to get rid of them. So here is where the story gets hairy, and I am not proud of what my son and I concocted together. Like criminals we took them to a city park, Roger releasing while I did a slow drive-by.

By then Roger had earned a reputation as the snake man, as he would walk around with this brightly coloured snake everywhere he went. The farm labourers working in the vineyards would bring him snakes. They brought him some kinda olive verbena snake. She was pregnant. The verbena laid her eggs and upon seeing this miracle in the fish tank, I decided they needed warmth and proceeded in cooking the poor babies under a heat lamp. Not a very bright mom.

He then had a water snake that fed on tadpoles. Roger would collect them and feed them to the snake. I never interfered. My family came to visit and found Roger with the snake in the bath, feeding tadpoles to his hungry charge.

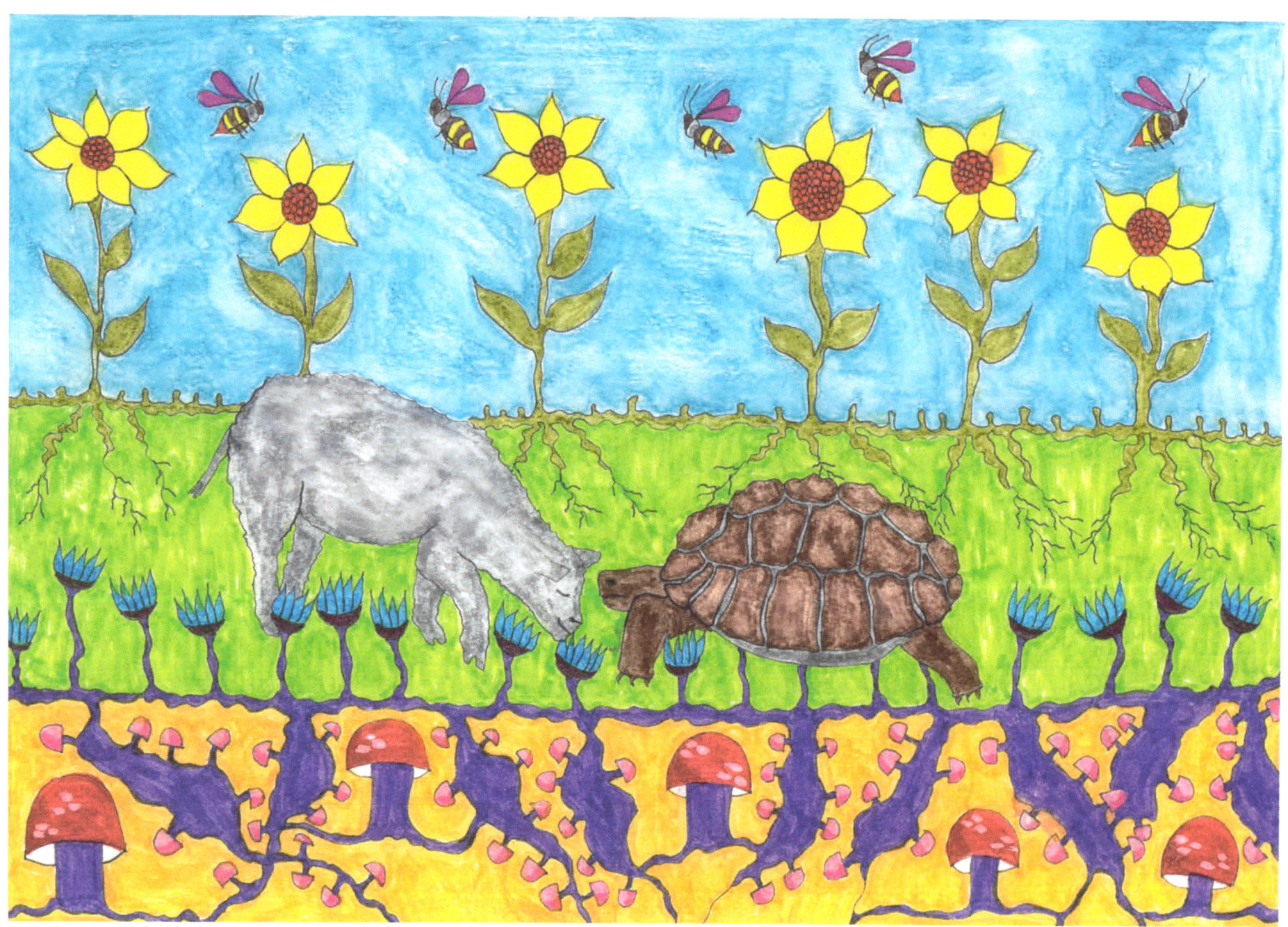

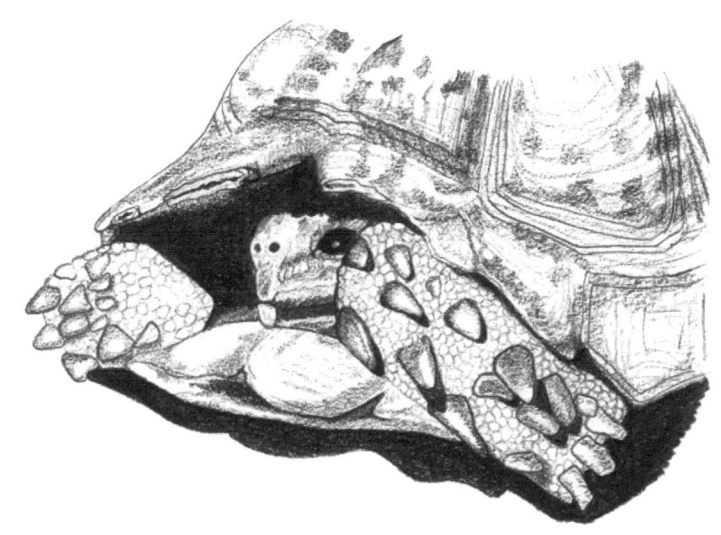

8

THE TORTOISE **&** WHEN SHIT HAPPENS

Our home was always open to any animal. Carolyn's boyfriend stopped some men carrying a heavy load, and lo and behold, a huge mountain tortoise was in their possession. In South Africa a tortoise is a delicacy to the locals, no matter that it took the poor thing years and years to get to a reasonable size.

This one was huge, probably 600cm high. He looked like a tank. Johan bought it off them for R50, as he knew where it was heading, and the tortoise then came to live with us. I fashioned a tortoise crossing about 30cm high at our gate leading to our stoep.

He was safe. All our friends had to step over the tortoise crossing. We would not see the tortoise for days, but he would walk through the house, down the steps on cue when friends were visiting. Where

he went when we could not find him was a mystery. He probably was chilling somewhere in the house.

My brother and some friends were visiting, and as per usual we were enjoying some gorgeous wine and braaiing. Next thing Wynand is moving in his chair. My brother is not a small man. He is a solid individual with calves the size of soccer balls. The tortoise was stuck under his chair and decided to go a-wandering, taking my brother with him.

In the middle of a braai we would often walk up to the dam for a swim. My friends enjoyed the freedom of walking amongst the vineyards, swimming at night with just the moon as our light.
That specific night, Lyncttc and a few went swimming, while I looked

after the meat cooking. It was rather dark that night. As they came back, their laughter and banter as light as the evening air, Lynette forgot about the tortoise crossing and I kid you not, fell on her boobs. I had never seen any woman fall on their boobs. And good friend that I was, I packed up laughing. She was not amused.

THE STORY OF BABE

Another lamb entered our lives. Roger had been asking for a lamb to raise for some time now, but I knew no one that could assist.
A very good friend, Jean, and I went on a road trip. She had hurt her back in a horrible freak accident and she was healing. In the spring we have a natural occurrence. A flower spectacle that plays itself out every year, and people from all over the world come to witness this event.

It happens in a sparsely populated area of the Karoo. Big sheep farms and little else. We had a wonderful time and on our return trip we went through a very isolated area.

For some time now we had noticed that even for these parts, no soul was around. Later on we discovered that everyone was at the meat festival in Calvinia, a small little town in the middle of everywhere. Minding our own business, my friend spotted a forlorn little lamb in a field with not an adult sheep anywhere to be seen. Being an animal lover herself, she pleaded with me to stop. I turned around and went into the field with the little lamb standing alone in isolation.

Now to catch the lamb...

Suddenly he jumped into action and bolted. Around, around the car we went, eventually able to capture the lively lamb. Jean was afraid he would be lunch on someone's table, and so we tried in vain to find the owner of this little lamb. Now how the hell do you find the owner when everyone is visiting the meat festival in Calvinia?

I gave her a stern sermon on stock theft, and in these parts as you could easily get shot. We ended up taking the lamb home. My son's face was precious. He could not believe it. They became inseparable. He named it Babe, and Babe slept next to Roger every night. The school phoned me to say that the lamb had to stay home. Okay.

He loved this lamb, but I could not get the lamb's diarrhoea under control. I gave him probiotics but nothing would work. Waking up Roger in the morning, he would look at me with green stuff all over his hair. One morning the lamb did not want to wake up. The agony was horrendous.

My son took the death of this little lamb very badly. Every day after school he would come home and build a fire. I clearly remember it was in the winter when the vineyards are bleak and grey. Half burnt-out fires littered the garden. It was indeed a very sad time. My son mourned this loss and it was heart-breaking.

WHAT THE HELL IS GOING ON?

Not so long after, Roger became lethargic. It was a big effort to get up. He lay on the couch day in and day out. I could not understand what was going on. In an exasperated moment I said he was like a giant sloth on the couch. I regret that.

I took him to the doctor. Many times. Months passed and I could not find out what was going on. The doctors said I was paranoid. Just normal teenage stuff. December rolled on with no improvement. Now it was tick bite fever and we medicated Roger. I was talking to a good friend about all this when she mentioned that it sounded to her like diabetes. What? We had just been to the doctor.

I immediately phoned and asked if they had tested his sugar. No. OMW. Really? The easiest test! We ended up in hospital as his sugar was off the charts. It took a whole weekend in hospital to get his sugar down so they could actually measure it. My son was diabetic. Type 1. You could have hit me over with a feather.

His body was devouring itself. He weighed a mere 35kg. Being so close to him, I had not noticed his weight loss. It was horrendous. I battled with the absolute randomness of this. True to Roger's spirit, he took ownership and started injecting himself in hospital.

Until today I still have my days where I cannot come to terms with the random events. Doctors are divided on the reason, some say a virus, others say a dramatic event, and I cannot help but think the loss of his lamb had something to do with his diabetes.

SAMURAI ROGER

Our life continued and the traumatic event lost its colour. Gardening became an integral part of our existence. We were spoiled for choice and had the ultimate dream and luxury of walking into the garden and picking that night's supper. On such a night, I sent Roger out to pick some broccoli... Let my story in the Bolander pick up from here...

PICKING BROCCOLI IS NOT THAT STRAIGHTFORWARD
BOLANDER, 27 JANUARY 2010

I know if you have ever met Accident, but the other day my son introduced me to him and he sent me to the Stellenbosch Medi Clinic. I don't like Accident, he's an opportunistic meaner.

And Broccoli likes Accident. They hang out in my garden together. My son was minding his own business little while ago, on his merry way to cut some broccoli for supper from the garden – and being 14 years old, he had to choose the biggest knife in the house (which I have no shortage of – other women buy shoes, I buy knives).

And with a dramatic swoop that would make any samurai warrior green with envy, he not only cut the broccoli, but also the top of his left writing hand, severing two tendons and cutting right down to the marrow. Oh, how Accident rejoiced!

So after scolding him for bleeding all over the floor and chasing him out of the house, we paid Stellenbosch Medi Clinic a visit. And there I found Angels. The staff at the emergency were remarkable. Whether it helped that we were the only emergency case, I couldn't tell: all I know is that they were absolutely wonderful, efficient and completely competent.

As my son is diabetic, we were immediately sent to the orthopaedic section, and there we found more Angels. My son had his tendons sewn back together by a very patient and talented doctor (who did not scold me for allowing my son to use the biggest knife in the house), and by midnight I could leave my son in the hands of the Angels.
So now I have to thank Accident for the wake-up call and for introducing me to a bunch of Angels.

Back to broccoli – one of my favourite vegetables, versatile, tasty and loaded with all kinds of goodness. I plant broccoli right through the year; try to rotate (although I am naughty and don't always follow my own advice), and watch out for the dreaded white butterfly that oh so innocently could wipe out your entire crop with her banded children.

I just squash them; I have no mercy.

Editor's Note: I no longer plant broccoli in the summer as the cabbage butterfly, although beautiful, annihilates any brassica.

And talking about no mercy, I will now explain the most effective way of dealing with that vicious intruder, the snail.

Step 1: Put on some gum boots.

Step 2: Wait for half an hour after sundown and water your garden – this is called entrapment.

Step 3: Wait about an hour or so. Inspect regularly for the intruders.

Step 4: When they arrive en masse, stomp all over them.

I find this method organic. It has the added benefit of releasing tension. All in all a winner.

A VERY TASTY SALAD WITH BROCCOLI:

Steam well-washed broccoli and cauliflower, and even some sliced carrots, until al dente.

Allow to cool.

Chop an onion with green leaves or use spring onion leaves (you really need to start planting some onions)

Mix some cream with organic Greek yogurt, add some chopped garlic to taste (lots of that). Add salt and pepper.

Marinate the whole lot for about at least two hours before serving.

And by the way, my boat of plenty is doing fabulously.

Editor's Note: This poor boat. It was a project of my brother and Roger.

Ok wait wait wait. Let me begin with my brother Wynand....

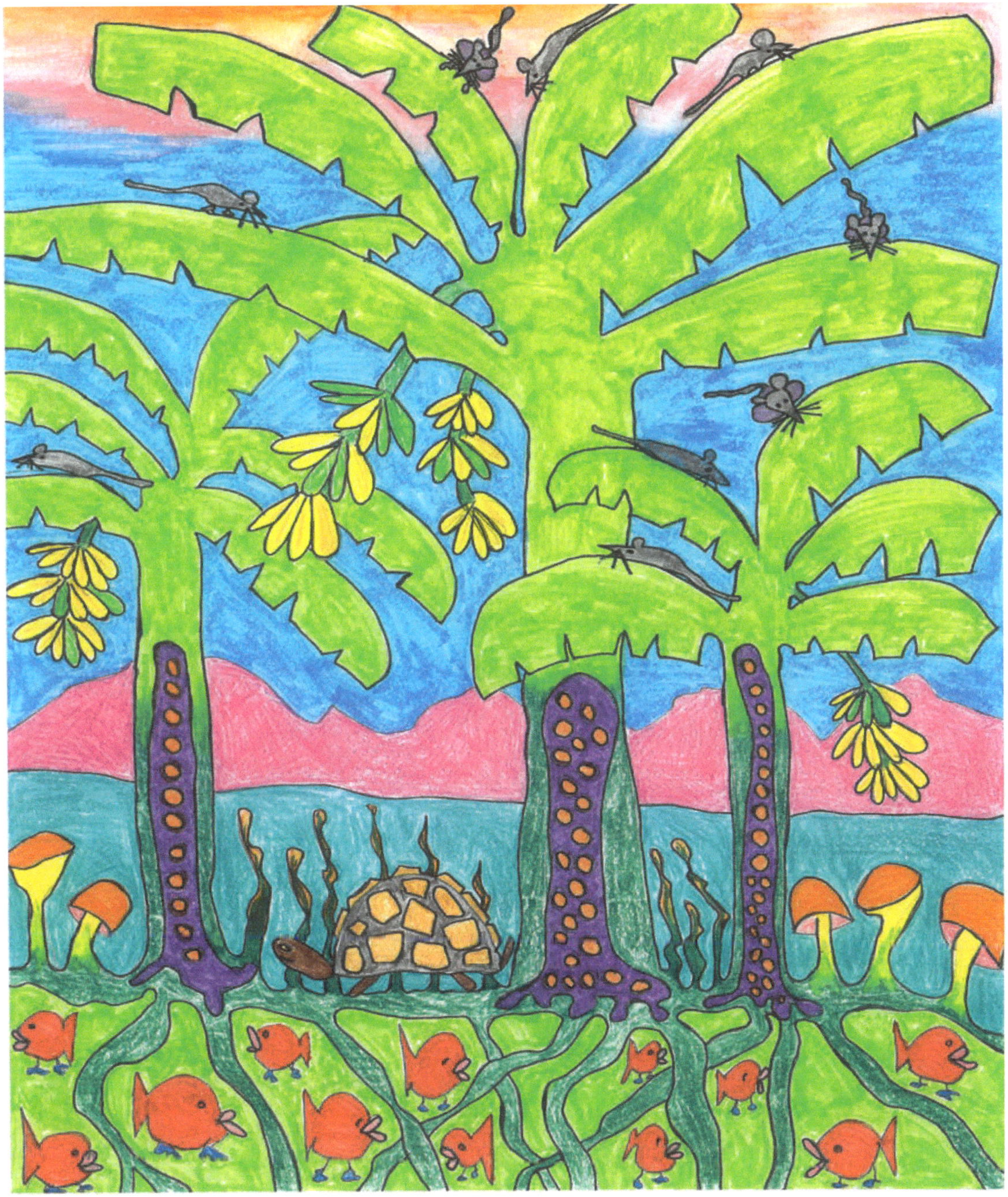

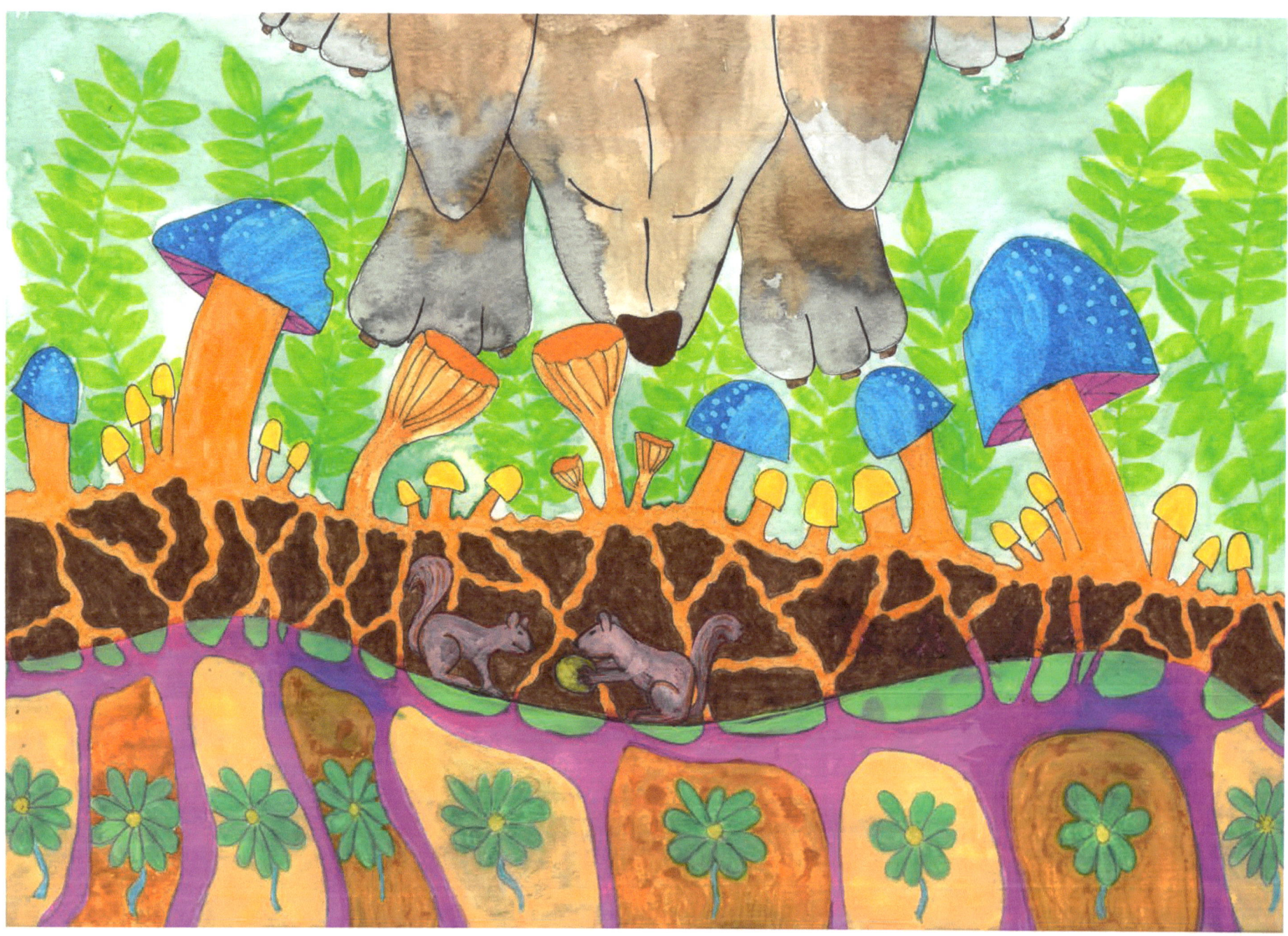

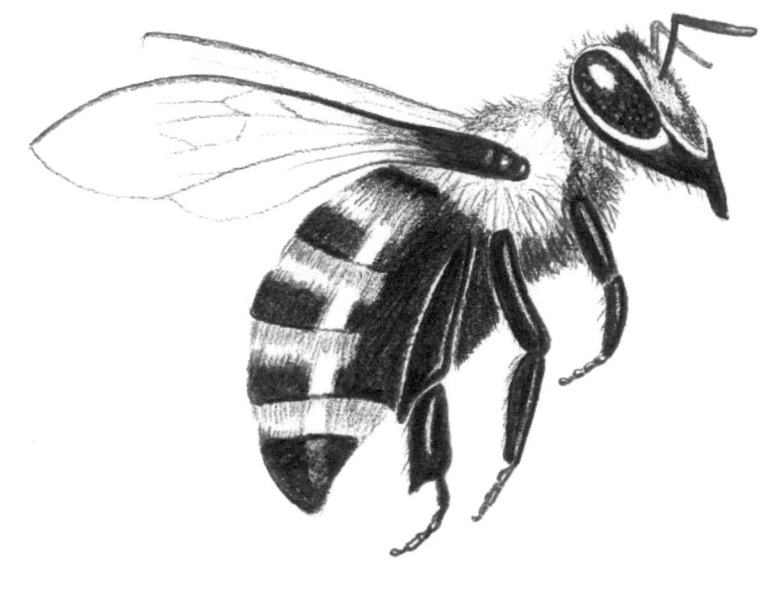

9

DA CASE OF DA SIBLING

I was the youngest of three siblings. Wynand the eldest, and my middle sister, Michelle. I get along well with both, and can best describe my relationship with my brother as lovingly exasperating. I can get so cross with him, and of course vice versa, but the love is always there.

When I returned with Roger after spending 8 years in America, I had no clue how I would make a living, as I had been out of the law profession for so long, and spent my time in America fine-arting it up. So my brother came to fetch us at our family home in Port Elizabeth.

When I left, I gave my mom strict instructions to look after several bonsais, thinking it would be an 18-month stint, but which then turned into 8 years. She did look after them, they were alive, but no longer bonsai. Spindly beyond recognition, clinging to life, the trees resembled... really hungry people. That's the only way I can describe them, starving and malnutritioned.

I could not leave without them, and vowed that I would plant them when I found my roots, symbolically rooting together. So off we went with these long, thin trees in Wynand's Landrover. One of these trees was the nameless tree, and subsequently with Google in our lives, I found out that it is from Australia, and how it grew between us and the Shellews, our neighbours, when nobody even knew where Australia was, would be anyone's guess.

I carted the trees from place to place, moving several times until I found my roots on the farm, and could finally release my precious trees that I had nurtured as a young girl, their roots free at last. The nameless tree is now a giant and every year we are blessed with mounds and mounds of pink bells.

Wynand was ever-present in our lives, visiting the farm often. He was very fond of Roger and played a big part in his development. Until today he remembers things about Roger that I have long forgotten.

So back to the boat of plenty. It was an epoxy project. A lot of yelling and hours and hours of labour later, a flat-bottomed, blue canoe type water craft saw the light of day. Roger looked like he had weathered a nightmare.

Wynand invited his friends to witness its release in the sea of all places, bottle of champagne and all. It looked dicey. My brother is a solid man and I am not too thin myself. He gave one look at its seaworthiness, and sent Roger and I on its maiden voyage. Now a flat-bottomed boat and the sea are not mates. We floundered around like a duck with one clipped wing and called it a day. The boat came to the farm, and I subsequently planted stuff in it.

My brother was always one for projects. There was always a lot of yelling involved, with many differences of opinion. For years I was left with a rather large (portable, he said) triangular, hefty metal cage. It was a welding project. It was supposed to be a chicken pen that you could move from place to place.

As stubborn as I, he would not relent on the size and weight. I was stuck with an awkward pyramid of steel which irritated the shit out of me for years, until my prince cut it in half and carted it away, which was a few months back. Ja, Ja, Ja did you read that... I found my prince but that is a very long story. And I will need a drink... bit early for that now, so best left for later.

The years passed and we were very happy. Roger inherited my "I-can-do-anything attitude" and the farm became his lab. As a school project, he decided to investigate gun powder. He took my old 70's toaster, used the curly whirly wires and other things and made himself of all things a bazooka, with an electric ignition thingy which really did fire something that looked pretty lethal. It was all very mysterious to me and I left him to his own devices.

Of this time I wrote the following article:

HUNGRY FOR THE GENTLE TIMES
BOLANDER, 15 SEPTEMBER 2010

I have a mortar and pestle. It is beautiful – heavy cast-iron with white enamel. I have lovingly milled my spices and herbs over an extended time, causing it to exude an exotic aroma.

Well, that's all gone now. I found my beloved mortar and pestle in my son's room with something that resembles gunpowder in it. The tragedy!

So, I have apparently entered the phase which I shall call, the explosive years. I fear I may have run out of hair to turn grey. My son has always shown a latent love of anything that can explode, blow up (there is a difference), burn and generally just disintegrate with a lot of smoke. Now it's under the guise of a school project. Heaven forbid. I wonder if I am going to make it. I wonder also, who invented the mortar and pestle? Such a simple design, yet spectacular in its effectiveness. Sure, I can go to the Internet, but it's much more fun to wonder.

This year I planted broad beans, halfway through the winter, escaping the aphids that find their tips irresistible and have supplied (an old) La Masseria (in a new location) called Agriturismo – on the R44 between Somerset West and Stellenbosch – combining slow food with negligible carbon footprint, the idea being that the deli and restaurant is supplied by small farmers in the immediate vicinity (like me), ensuring the freshest of ingredients and as a bonus an ever-changing and flexible menu.

And for the first time I have planted baby spinach, it is incredible. It's not a huge plant, and starts well with general seeding. But the taste... and this is apparently what the Italians call spinach. What we eat as spinach, is chard.
And cosmically, I have planted what the Italians like, as if I knew that I would meet up with the folks at La Masseria.

I arrived the other day with a basket of veggies and there was Micky making gnocchi. Now, I have never attempted to make gnocchi and as she rolled the delicate little balls on a flat, grooved, wooden ladle, I vowed not to try.

Some things are better left to the experts, but it was as if the day had come to a standstill, a wonderful feeling of "everything is going to be fine" settled on my brow and I wondered at her beautiful skill, unaware of the awe I was feeling.

There is a definite hunger for the ways of a gentler time, when rolling gnocchi was an everyday occurrence, and good healthy food was all there was to eat. And now I am going to pick some broad beans.

Am I glad that I had typing at school. Just saying.

I enjoyed writing quirky stories immensely as it gave me quick, creative satisfaction. The gardens expanded and became a jungle of plant species. Somewhere along the way I made a decision to only plant what we could eat. The birds did their bit, depositing fig seeds in the most unexpected places which I left to grow.

I discovered a new guava tree the other day, and unless I am starting to become seriously forgetful as I could never be that drunk to not remember planting it, I attributed it to a friendly bird. Over the years I became one with my garden, hearing the birds call when a snake was at their nests. The garden vibrated at a higher, frenzied pitch, I could be anywhere and I would know something was wrong.

Dogs were constant companions, and true to spirit we had to have many dogs. Not one or two. No, let's have three Great Danes and a whole swetterjoel[18] of others.

Of the dogs in our lives, I wrote:

EARTHNOTES IN A BASKET
BOLANDER, 29 SEPTEMBER 2010

This weekend I was driving with a basket full of veggies to my vet. I have an extraordinary vet. It may have something to do with the fact that I have seven dogs, two cats, 11 pot-bellied pigs and a selection of other animals.

And for 13 years he has lovingly cared for them – and recently seen the fall of my beloved and legendary alpha Great Dane male, Sam – and so has come to know this quirky client.

Recently I presented him with my newest edition (no matter that I have been retrenched for two years!), Avalanche the husky inherited from my brother (in Abu Dhabi) and his beautiful daughter (in England).

To explain the situation I said simply, as a good friend of mine does: "Nature does not tolerate a vacuum".

And all was understood between moi and my vet: a relationship akin to family. And he is now, as I am writing, climbing Kilimanjaro with this wife. What amazing people touch our lives?

To come back to my basket of veggies that I was taking to this remarkable man (kind eyes – what can I say – I love my vet). So, this basket of veggies, beside me in my two-seater bakkie, and I realized that if my son was coming along, he would be sitting on a crate on the back of my bakkie. What? I am serious! Such heavenly scent.

The tantalising aroma of earth emanating from this basket. It is akin to the smell of procreation. When connected to your soil, there is instant recognition of the basics of life, the life force. What a privilege. My most honourable and sacred duty is to inspire those who have lost the scent.

Do yourself a favour: next you have a spare moment, go into your garden and pull something out of your soil. Close your eyes and smell the heavenly scent.

Allow your heart to somersault. And think of planting something useful. It's easy. Take care of the soil, create a haven for organisms to grow, and you too can brag with a healthy, simple yet incredibly scrumptious salad.

My son and I are hosts to a delightful German volunteer. In Germany, every young man has to do a year of voluntary social service. So

Dennis, through the Waldorf School, has fallen on my household, and what a beautiful young man, full of the wanderlust of a foreigner in Africa.

I find myself looking at us in a different way, as if standing outside of our nation – and what I see, strikes me.

We are a unique race, strong. Our women rising to the occasion, our men passionate in their convictions, our children exploring new horizons.

I am part of the positive life force of this country. I will not buckle. We are good. Let no one take that away from us.

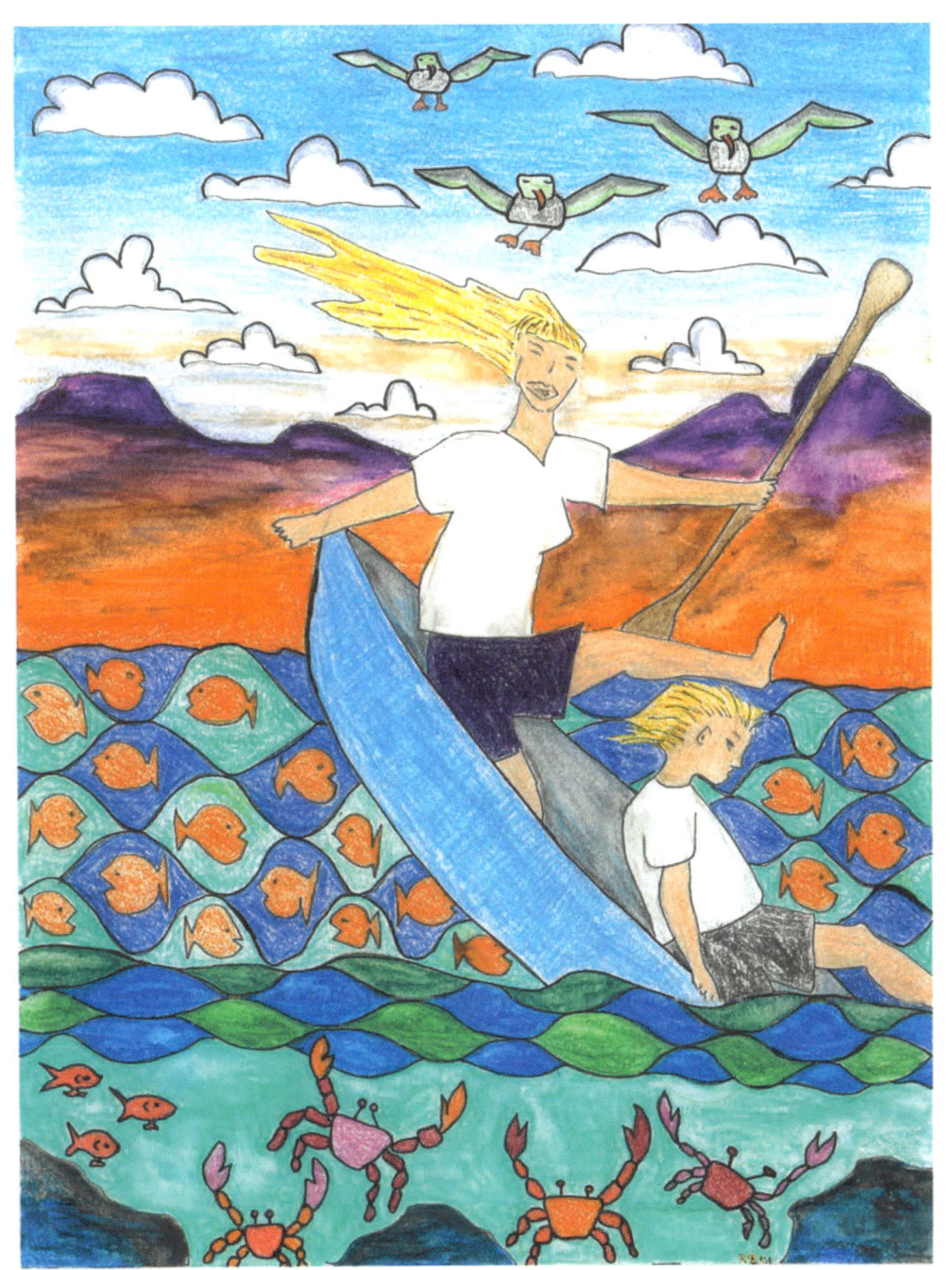

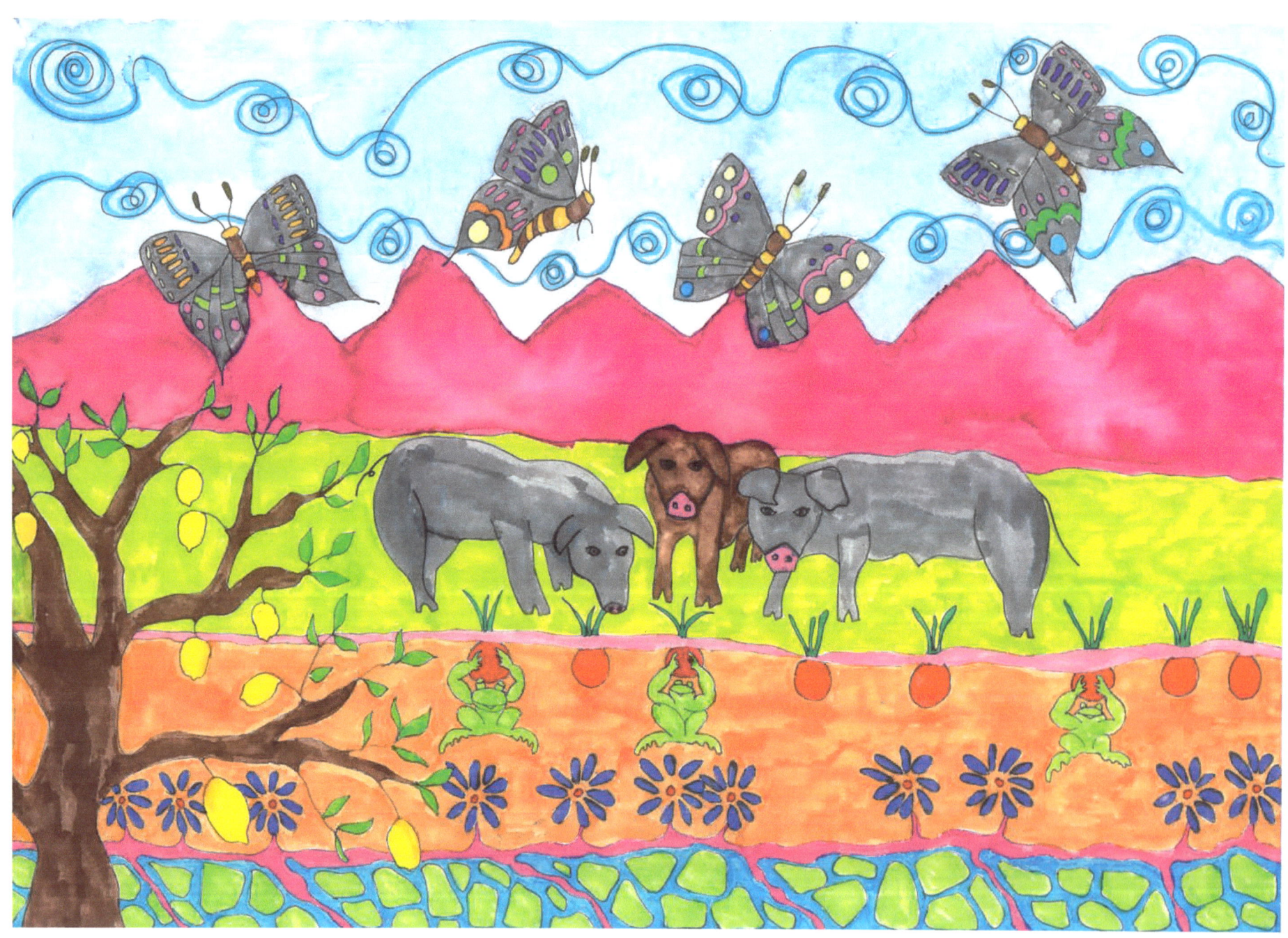

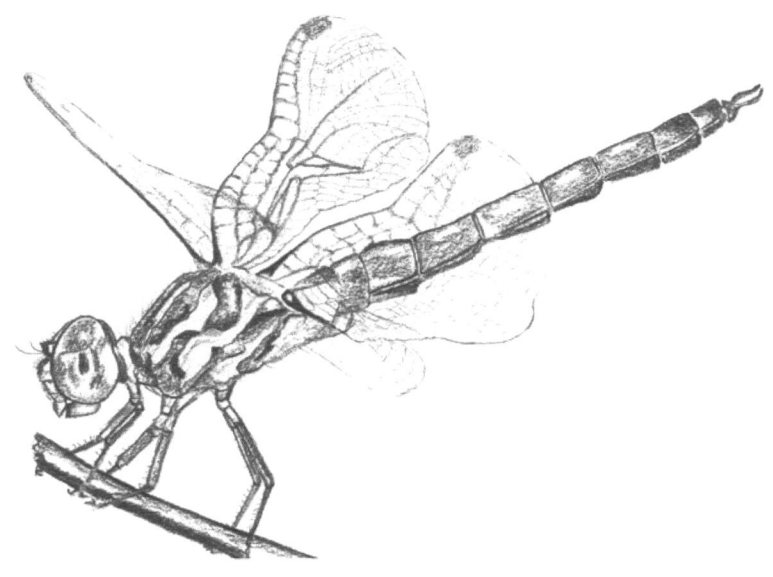

10

MAKING THE MOST

I became a serious gardener. As Roger was now a Type 1 Diabetic I wanted to make sure that we had the best of ingredients to work with. Trial and error, school fees paid in the form of rookie errors, saw new knowledge born from experience. And so I became a bit of an expert in a lot of stuff. At one point I lost my day job. Oops. Not good.

VOYAGES OF THE HEART: TO NAPIER & BEYOND
BOLANDER, 20 OCTOBER 2010

It always amazes me how your life can take on an entirely different colour when you strap on your boots and go bundu[19] bashing. After my retrenchment, I decided to live by my wits (those that are still at my disposal) and I have had such an enriching experience that to say

it has been fun will be an understatement equal to stating, say ' this is a very mild winter ' when huge old trees are flying all over the place. To keep us in food, I have increased my vegetable garden and now have three relatively big gardens – and in the process of keeping them clean and what not, have shed (not lost – because by George I do not want to find them again) a few extra kilograms, maybe 10.

So forget about watching your weight, just spend more time in your garden, and by that I means not as a manger, but as a labourer and you will be lighter in spirit and body. In need of some cash, I have also started a sauce business, and this has led me to some wonderful folk who attend organic markets as traders.

Recently my Portuguese friend and I had the opportunity to visit

Dragonfly farm, a goat farm in Napier. This peaceful place, with hundreds of goats as tame as dogs, is home to Jacqui and Brenda, voted best female farmers in 2009.

Their hospitality is formidable and their goats cheese divine. They live a simple life, no matter that Brenda was a hot New York photographer for many years and Jacqui a selfless NGO-type in Switzerland. The fact is, they choose to live the simple life, with their animals around them and their veggie gardens.

Theirs is to be envied, that simple decision to follow the heart. We left them with a lightness of being (and two healthy pigs, intrepid farmer that I am. Of course we had to stop at Caledon for a pit stop, and when we returned to Stellenbosch, it was late and pitch black on the farm.

Needless to say the pigs slept in my kitchen, uncomfortable in their confinement, a makeshift airline dog kennel and no-one could get any shuteye. Have you ever heard the noise uncomfortable pigs make? Nobody was impressed with anybody.

And so spring has descended on us, typical of the Cape, with stops and starts. I am busy importing loads and loads of black gold (manure for the unenlightened) and will allow my soil to do its thing for a few weeks.

It is this waiting period that seems endless, same as those last few days before birth, the waiting for something to arrive. I distinctly remember sitting in the rocking chair I insisted on and murmuring over and over like a mantra: "jy moet hieruit"[20] and then, when it does finally arrive, you are not sure if you really want it. That is, the summer, of course!

Somehow we survived my retrenchment with the help of many friends stopping by with a bag of dog food, my brother helping financially. My good friend Selma joined the sauce business, Maidens Tongue, herself heavily pregnant. Both of us are not afraid of hard work. And boy did we work hard. Her mother became ticked off with me for expecting her to still cook and to be honest I can't believe I did that. Our sauce business did not make it, and our dreams were a sticky mess.

Somehow life always continues and I found my stream again, working in the corporate world. Yuk! I had a brand-new company car, and Roger and I were fine. Back on track. I had met my prince but things were complicated. That tale a bit later.
I was now a serious gardener. Just in case you missed that. The gardens were lush and produced so much. I branched into all kinds of fruit trees... ah lol, branched.

Anyhow, my life was full of adventure as I met a new best friend, let's call her Cindy and she needs some protection. She was impossible. Tall, blond, loud, beautiful, huge heart.

Did I mention she was loud? The moment I stepped into my corporate job I saw her. We became fast friends. As wild in spirit as I am but with an added advantage, she could really drive. Like rally type driving, and we both had brand new company cars. That set the tone for many adventures with her as the driver, and what we did and where we went is rather left to the imagination. She may get fired. I swear, that girl!

One story I have to tell. She was in the technical team and I was in sales. So when people did not know the hell how to paint, we ended up attending to their stupidity. One such call was most definitely a road trip far. Road trip!!!

We timed it well to coincide with a weekend, which saw us visit her dad and his girlfriend, about 300km away. The road trip took us through the Karoo. Our kinda roads. Long and lonesome. The car sang.

We opened our windows to the open space of South Africa and found ourselves racing through kilometres and kilometres of Spekboom [21]. The pure air hit us as divers sucking on their oxygen tanks in the privacy of their homes, while Dolly Parton and Kenny Rogers were belting out Islands in the Stream. It was legendary. A natural high not induced by alcohol. How refreshing.

After concluding our official business, we went to visit the old folks and as they had limited space, I offered to sleep in my brand new bakkie, the fanciest 4x4 double cab I had ever owned. The seats were leather so I concluded it could only be comfortable. Duh! Mistake number one.

I had no clue how the alarm system operated, and after a whole lot of giggling and shushing (we are in a very small security complex) induced by a lot of wine, I locked myself in for the night. Not very bright. I had such a big wee. That half-way mark after a bottle of wine. The damn alarm and these nobbies I still have to figure out. The closest and deepest thing I could find was my safety helmet. Necessity is the mother of all solutions.

QUACK QUACK

Always looking for more animals to keep, and more plants to plant, I ended up with an idea to keep ducks. In a jiffy I dug a pool, cemented it and made another enclosure. Now to find the ducks. My previous experience with ducks ended in mass murder, as I made the mistake of buying some Quackers. Now they are called Quakers for a very specific reason. They quack and there is no stopping them. The most irritating sound any animal can make. To make things worse I had the bright idea to build their enclosure very close to the house. The incessant noise drove me crazy. And they stink. Nope.

MID-LIFE CRISIS: WHAT CRISIS?
BOLANDER, 8 APRIL 2015

I am getting to the age when my mid-life crisis is overdue (I am, after all, heading for year 51 and I am afraid it may have missed me completely).

I was so looking forward to becoming completely ridiculous. And throwing caution to the wind and buying something quite outrageous, like a horse or something equally crazy.

But instead, I took on another three rescue dogs, then went to Hopefield and bought five wild Muscovy ducks. And that, my friends, was the extent of it.

Well, so I think, but maybe... just maybe, my crisis is waiting for me around the next corner...

To be fair to my (hopefully looming but very shy) midlife crisis, the term 'midlife crisis' just doesn't do it justice. Kind of gives it a very negative feel, like it's something bad.
I have a very good friend who has been in a full-blown midlife crisis (plus some additions) for nearly five months. It's awesome.

Well perhaps for me, the outsider, looking in. The range of emotions and internal struggle leads me to the conclusion that this condition should actually be called 'a re-evaluation of your life lived thus far'. That doesn't sound exciting, but in essence that is what a midlife crisis is. And to be sure, you have to have lots of money to experience a crisis of this magnitude. Do you know how much a horse costs? Not to mention a Bugatti. My word. Only the rich can experience a full blown re-evaluation.

The rest must be happy with the gnashing of teeth that coincides with a midlife crisis (or a few extra dogs and some fowl).

But to go back to my mini crisis: five wild Muscovy ducks in two cardboard boxes, the big male separated from the girls in the back of my Toyota Corolla, in between my computer, safety gear and other paraphernalia of my working life. And I just know the character of Muscovy ducks. Harde gat[22]! Ten to one, they will try their level best to escape.

And I can hear the male is upset, really upset. So I turn off to Malmesbury, and as I head down that long stretch where the speed camera is, I hear the box overturn - and I can just imagine Muscovy doo doo all over my boot.
And it's not just any doo doo. Muscovies do it in a very deliberate way. It's more or less like Spiderman shooting out his web.
In my mind's eye I see my computer and said paraphernalia covered in big, huge 'blertse'[23]. Nasty.

So I stop at the top of this long downhill and open the boot just a wee bit, because I know how crafty these birds are – and before I can say knife, the big male is out and there he goes, with me in tow.

And that day I chose to wear a very bright pink jacket. With long blond hair flying behind me in the wind... down Malmesbury's long downhill in hot pursuit.
The males wings had been clipped, thank heavens, but as soon as I got close to him, he gave me a sardonic look over his magnificently iridescent, feathered shoulder and flew a few tantalising meters ahead. Really spiteful.

You try to catch a Muscovy male down a massive straight downhill with no natural barriers.

In desperation I started flagging down motorists. At this stage I was upgraded to a spectacle. Motorists were openly gawking at the sight they beheld.

Red face, pink jacket, out of breath, dishevelled and seriously agitated, and sweating buckets, at that stage in the chase, I was not a pretty sight – with very imaginative and colourful language to boot.

Eventually I managed to corner him in the only piece of brush, but I needed help. And guess who stops to offer help?

An ambulance man, driving a real ambulance, nonchalant as if he always stops for a woman chasing a Muscovy duck down a very long hill.

I was so grateful.

It ended well. The Muscovy duck is still alive and did not find his way into a pressure cooker as I promised, but instead fathered 13 ducklings, of which 12 survived and are now grown.

My midlife crisis, I think...

Yup I'm not making this all up.

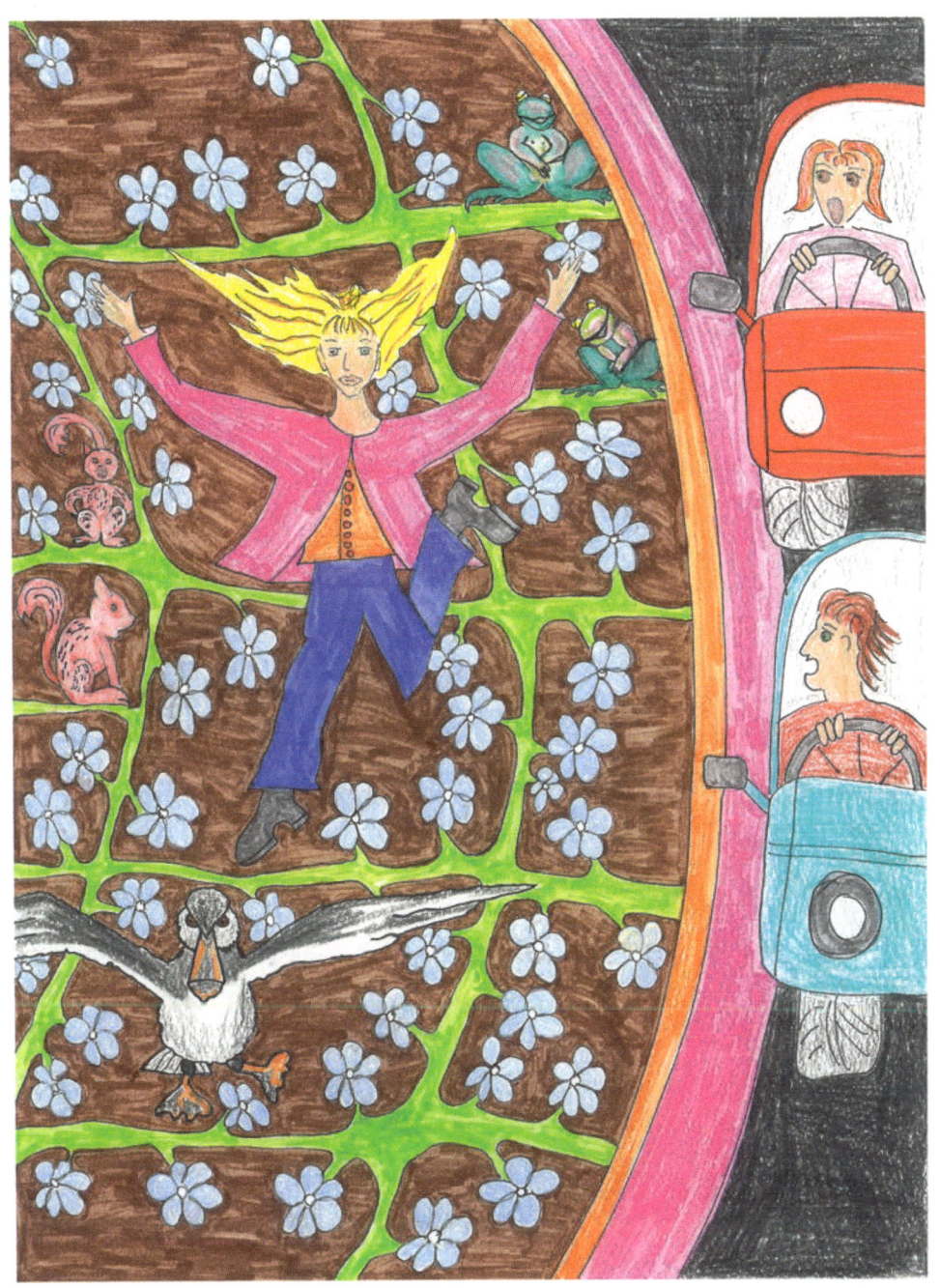

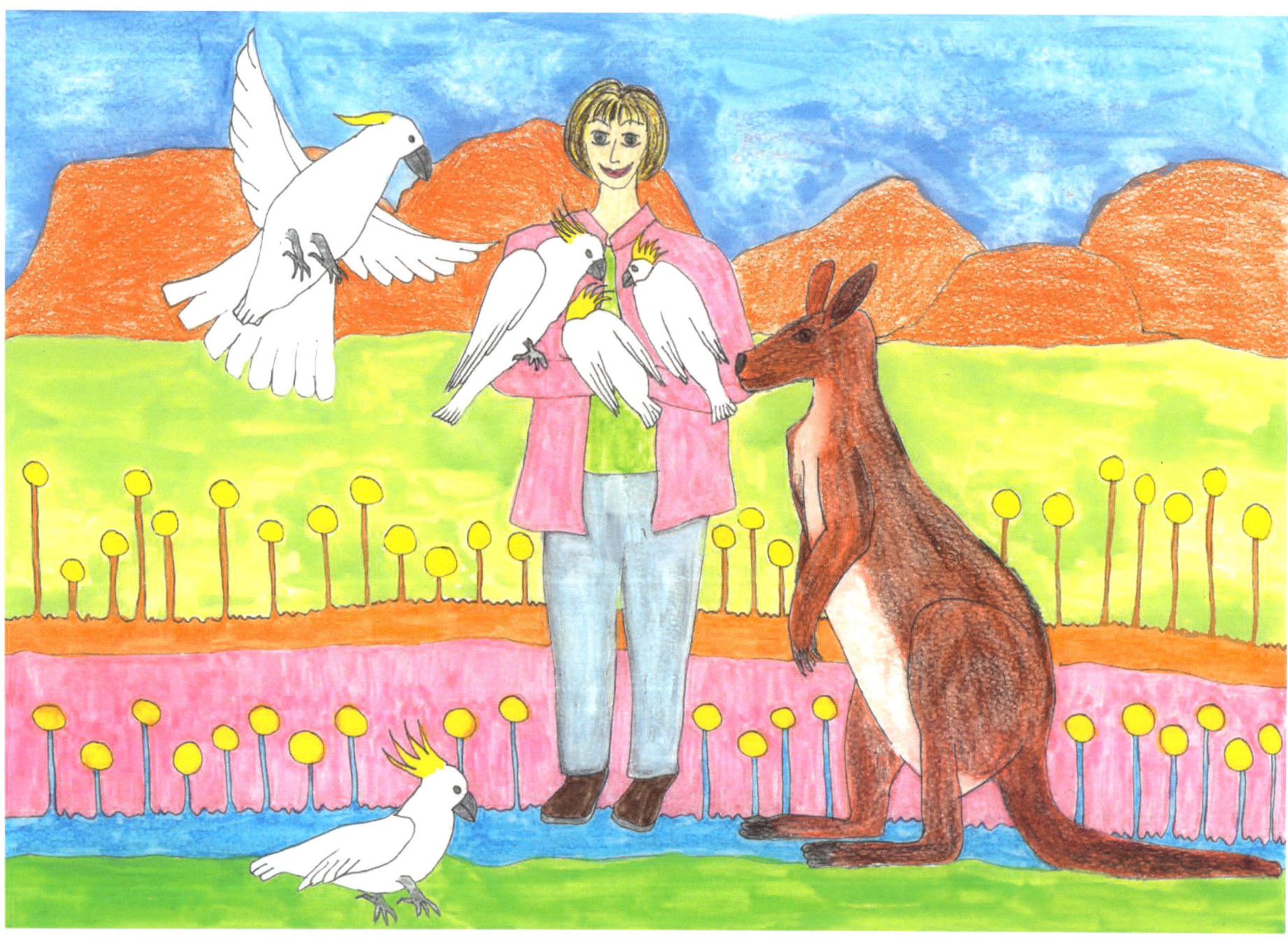

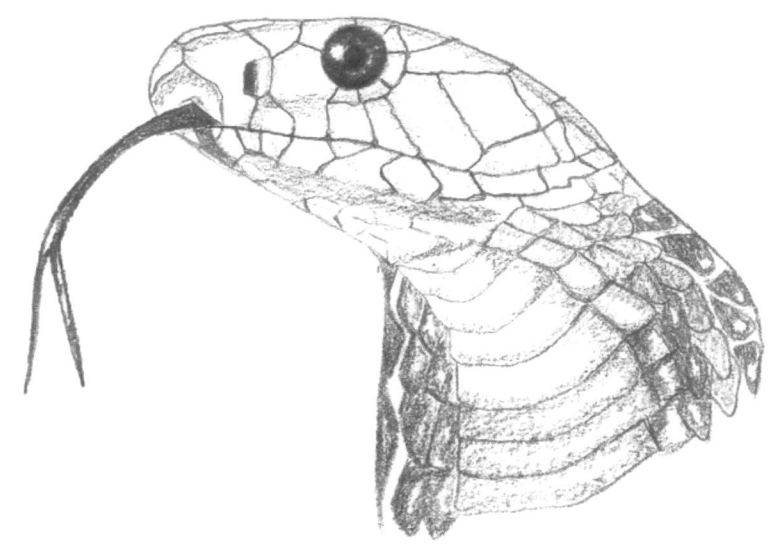

11

DOWN UNDER WITH MY SISTER

Very different from Wynand and I. Michélle has a brilliant mind and a heart of gold. I can wax on and on about my sister. She is in Australia and I went to visit her. I had not seen her for many, many years. Near the end of my visit, we were having lunch with her friends and words just fell out of my brain. I grabbed a napkin and wrote:

MEMOIRS OF MY JOURNEY DOWN UNDER
BOLANDER, 1 JULY 2015

About five years ago my son and I made a list and stuck it to the fridge. It was a list of wishes. Some big and ambitious – like a herd of Nguni cattle, or a mushroom farm – and some humble, like a pair of gloves, sheets, lawnmower.

There were fanciful wishes and practical wishes. And so with the years we could cross out most wishes, but a few hardy ones remained.

Out of the blue my sister from Australia phoned: envisaging a long conversation I made myself comfortable at the long kitchen table. She wanted me to visit her in Australia, all expenses paid including the plane ticket – and as we were excitedly discussing my visit, I looked over at the fridge, and forgotten amongst all the scribbles and crossed out wishes, stood out the wish: Australian visit.

One that I never thought would be possible. I was in tears, and two months later I found myself boarding Emirates Airlines off on my adventure.

What an experience. Firstly, I ate my way through Australia. I am what we call in Afrikaans, a 'lekkerbek'[24]. Food is not only there to feed my body, but most importantly, to feed my soul.

I plan my meals with as much care as some people plan their retirement. It is not merely a 'grab what is available' – it is a carefully calculated choice of nutrition versus pleasure.

The older I get the more careful the planning, for I am of the unfortunate disposition that a mere glance at food will result in weight gain in the oddest of places.

I had melt in the mouth macaroons, a taste unlike anything I can describe. Wonderful, wholesome hummus served with beautifully spiced lamb mince, accompanied with marinated chillies, pickles and olives.

Ah the flavour. I had succulent, robust lamb, the flavour much stronger than ours, kangaroo steak (reminiscent of rabbit crossed with ostrich), beautifully presented Asian fusion food, each plate a visual masterpiece.

I saw the magnificent city of Melbourne, an odd mixture of old English brookie lace intermingled with super modern architecture. I travelled on tram, bus and ferry. A public transport system always on time, scrupulously clean and safe.

On my last day I met a great storyteller. My sister belongs to a very unusual church; it is actually not a church as much as a movement. A movement under Jewish to accept the new testament alongside the old, a very radical concept. The rabbi of this mixed Gentile and Jewish Shul, is the son of the man who owned the Hole in the Wall Hotel in Somerset West, Ronnie Hirsh. Small world.

So in a very blonde moment I missed my flight home. At Shul, I met other members of this prestigious club (ja, also blonde), hence the following story:

Lucy is a buxom 50-odd blonde who had to fly somewhere, let's call it Brisbane (details get caught up in the fuzz of my brain).

Firstly, she was overweight (her luggage, but yes also herself, slightly). Out comes all manner of clothing, the exact details I will spare you, with her father (remember she is over 50-something, so how old is he) sitting alongside with a disapproving face, while granddaughter and daughter are frantically ripping personal items from her luggage and stuffing it in the only thing they had, which was a small crate.

Eventually she boards the plane, but has the misfortune of sitting next to a very large lady. She foolishly decides to put on her support stockings in this confined space.

She got the one on, but the leg adjacent to the very large lady presented a problem. She could not just give her the leg and say; "Please put on my support stocking."

In the pursuing wrestle, unbeknownst to her, she popped a hernia in her side, apparently a sports injury many active, buxom women experience. Being ignorant of such matters, she thought she had pulled a muscle, be it in a very peculiar spot.

So here she is in the air, next to a very large lady, in excruciating pain with one leg supported, the other offending leg, supportless.

She grabbed the chair in front of her, groaning in very unladylike fashion, and pushed the offending sausage which had suddenly appeared in her side, back whence it came, and proceeded to wrestle the other support stocking in between unearthly groans of pain.

Next day she visited a doctor with her friend (also buxom). The doctor, wiry, thin and unfriendly with not a smidgen of sympathy: "It's a hernia, not a pulled muscle" – and then proceeds to notify her that she should lose some weight, and promptly informs her innocent, supportive friend that she could also do with losing some weight. How's that for two for the price of one?

At this stage of the story I felt like I had popped a hernia myself. What a funny woman. The story continues, but alas I am out of breath. A fabulous holiday filled with interesting people and places.

I saw kangaroos, ate kangaroo, a dingo swallowed my earring (another story), we nearly hit a koala bear languidly crossing the road, saw the outback (or part thereof) at a gallop and ate amazing food. I came upon a vast plain, so vast you could see the curvature of the earth (an illusion maybe). I witnessed a flock of cockatoos, a thousand strong, fly overhead.

They have dog breeds called cavoodle (cross between a cavalier spaniel and a poodle), retrodoodle (cross between a retriever and a poodle), labradoodle (yes, a cross between a lab and a poodle), and spoodle (cross between a spaniel and a poodle). These are real dogs, mind you. Here we would call them brakke (mongrels).

I saw not one single stray dog (they do apparently have some up north). I did not see a single beggar, nor a single homeless person (although I am sure they are there). No litter whatsoever.

They have honesty boxes. Farmers place vegetables on the side of the road and you can put your money in a box.
I ate gorgeous vegetarian food at a restaurant and all that was required

was a donation, if you could afford it.

At grocery stores, you scan your own products. Honesty, such a scarce commodity in our South Africa, taken for granted Down Under.

The last few days back in South Africa, I have been moving around with a heavy heart.

We are so far removed from the road that our beloved Mandela put us on.

Will we ever experience honesty as a way of living?

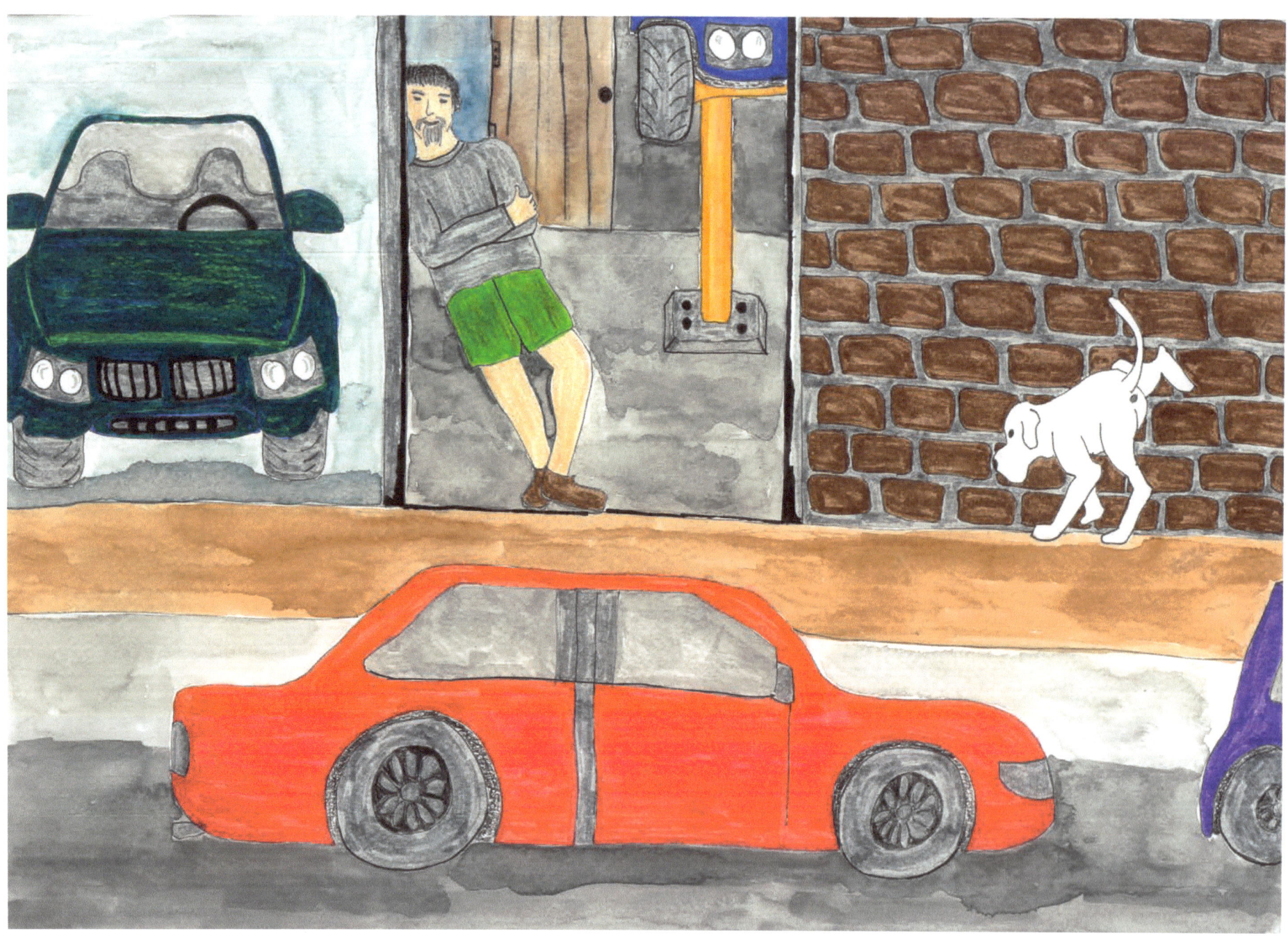

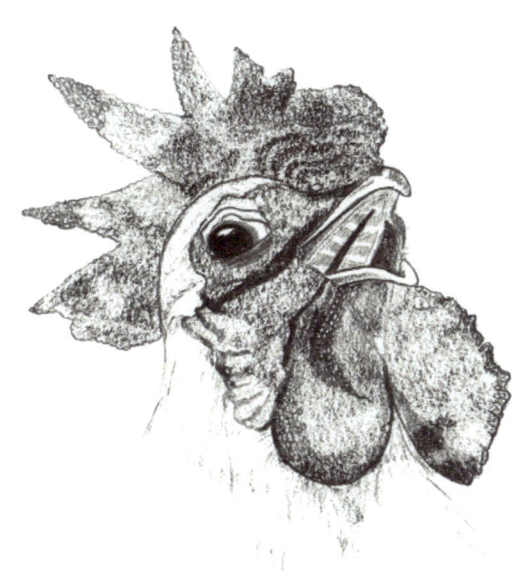

12
THE PRINCE

I was always on the road, consulting for paint companies which entailed a lot of driving. I enjoyed the freedom and saw a lot of out of the ordinary places in South Africa. Have you been to Koekenaap[25]? I have. There's a wind farm there. I had one fateful stint in a shop. The paint shop was battling and I was asked to assist. At that stage I had been on the road for many years, and I thought a break would be good.

I arrived early that morning in my customary big bakkie (a very nice diesel 3lt Ford Ranger truck). I had driven bakkies my entire life, with one exception: a badly chosen French car that was a disaster on wheels.

It was the lower part of Main Street, with many different businesses lining the road. Across from my new position was an automatic transmission business, a battery place and so forth.

After introducing myself, I went outside to check out the neighbourhood and low and behold, across from me stood trouble. He was leaning against the sliding door of the automatic transmission shop. And he was staring at me. He was masculine, my age, looked like a biker (and my mom always said they were trouble). Sexy as hell. My loins gave a twitch.

The attraction was instant. When Peter tells the story he says he saw my pink panties sticking out and that was that for him. The games began. Everyone in my shop knew what was going on, but Peter and I pretended that nothing was happening.

He would come over and buy a spray can of something. The man does gearboxes, what did he do with all the paint. As soon as he arrived, my assistant, Karina would call me to tend to the 'customer'. Every morning, we would come to work before anyone else, casually stroll outside with a mug of coffee, and try very hard not to see each other. That man can work on my transmission anytime!

The shop was floundering and I decided to entice the contractors with a braai.

Every Friday I would start up the fire. Karina's husband would braai, as in his mind no woman can braai. I am a very capable braaier[26], so this really grated my nerves.

Once, at one of Roger's camps, I was the only one that thought of bringing tongs. The kids were starving and I started cooking everyone's meat on a very rudimentary grid. My coals were sorted according to the different cuts and everything was cooking perfectly. Well, this dad came and took my tongs out of my hands...! I nearly floored him right there on the spot. I wrestled the tongs back and told him in no uncertain terms where to stick his non-existent tongs.

Karina's husband would stab the boerewors[27], juice spraying all over the place, and my irritation levels would be soaring. What kind of idiot stabs the wors (sausage)?

I had invited all of the businesses, and Peter was watching, the stabbing of the wors too much for him. Thankfully he took over. It gave us an opportunity to talk to each other and we discovered many commonalities.

We both loved cooking. Chicken a la king was his forte, and curry, mine. We both were adventurous. In many ways we were the same person. Our attraction was mind-blowing.

A slew of armed robberies were taking place on our street, and the battery people organized a meeting. We all sat in a big circle. He came in, chose the seat next to me and said: "I think I will sit next to the prettiest woman here." My engine revved.

The tension between us was unbearable. This went on for quite some time. How many paint cans he bought and what he did with them, I don't know. I asked Selma to give him the once over as my judgement was questionable. I had had disastrous luck with men, so I was not going to trust myself with this one. We went over with some kinda stupid car question and she gave me the ok.

After work with the street quiet and just the two of us there, I walked over to him, my shaky legs not agreeing with the other bits. He had the habit of having a whiskey before leaving. My strategy was going to be pure, straight Anita. I asked him;

"Are you available?"
He said: "No".
I heard a thud. I think my engine fell out. Just my luck.
I rallied: "Do you want to have fun?"
"Yes," he replied.
"Do you like kissing?" Yes.

I leaned forward and kissed this sexy man. I was a goner.
He was married. Bummer. Yes, living in separate rooms for years, but he was married. Fuck! My luck. Adult kids. So, so complicated. And our street was like Sewende Laan[28].

A freakin tammeletjie[29] of note. And I had my son to consider. He was 16. No fool. And we lived so closely with each other. I would have to tell him the truth.

A fun courtship ensued. We tried desperately to keep it a secret. Our love language was food. I would cook a beautiful curry for him and elaborately hide it in a box.

Mbelelo, the shop tinter had to deliver the box to keep Sewende laan fooled. Inside would be a love note with my special chicken curry, guaranteed to go straight for the heart and hopefully other bits and bobs.

The curry was luscious, rich and filled with passion.

LOVE CURRY

To set the mood play some sexy Barry White and
pour
yourself a glass of wine.

FRESH INGREDIENTS:

2 large onions, finely chopped
2 cloves of garlic, finely chopped
A twig of thyme
A good chunk of ginger, grated
4 fresh bay leaves
2 healthy branches of curry leaves (about 20 leaves)
3 chillies, chopped

SPICES:

1 tablespoon of turmeric
2 teaspoons coriander seeds, crushed

1 teaspoon black peppercorns, crushed
2 teaspoons cumin
1 teaspoon methi
1 tablespoon black mustard seeds
3 whole cloves
1 whole nutmeg, crushed
3 whole star anise
4 allspice
4 cardamom pods, crushed
Salt to taste

I nearly forgot the chicken, cut in pieces.

3-4 potatoes, washed and cut into pieces.
Saute the spices in oil. Do not burn. Sip some wine.

Add the fresh ingredients and saute until softened.

Add the chicken and potatoes and cover with chicken stock, a beer or some wine (not too much).

And now let the love happen. Slowly simmer for about an hour to two depending on how much wine you have had and if Barry is still playing.

Serve with rice, sambals, yogurt and fresh coriander leaves.

Not to be outdone, he would send his mechanic with a plate of chicken a la king. In full view of Sewende laan. Oh my word.
And so our courtship continued for many months. Food going to and through with my tinter and his mechanic. It was a very big deal for Peter as he loves his children and respects their mother. There

was no animosity between them. Just different paths so we went to inordinate lengths to keep our affair a secret.

It was important to me to test this man. I would be the other woman. Am I just another plaything? So I invited him to the farm on one of my single weekends.

I warned him about my mentally unstable dog, Apollo. "He will bite you," I said. Which was no exaggeration, as he had bitten a few of my friends. The front door would be unlocked. My cottage was a minefield of farm paraphernalia, a wall of leftover boxes from Maiden's Tongue lined the passage. Neatness was not my forte. There was probably some kind of baby animal on the kitchen table I was trying to save.

"Go through the lounge, through the kitchen, left and mind the step, and you will face three closed doors. Choose wisely." At the appointed hour I heard a car. The dogs barked. Car door closing. No cry of pain or snarling sounds. Mmh, what's wrong with Apollo? The front door opened and closed. So far so good. Now to negotiate my haphazard house. A few "Oh shits". A "fuck". He must have found the steps. He is close. My body was so tense you could play a song on it. I lay in anticipation, waiting for this virile, sexy man to open the right door. He did.

Years later I mentioned that I could not believe that Apollo did not bite him, and he sheepishly admitted to bringing with two healthy chunks of mince in both pockets. Crafty!

We were insanely jealous of each other. I had been working in a man's world all my adult life, so I have an easygoing relationship with men. I changed jobs and left the area. I was now working with Cindy, also single for a very long time. We enjoyed each other's company

and became fast friends. We spent a lot of time together as Peter was still committed to his other life.

Ridiculous jealousy plagued our relationship. He would accuse me of torrid love affairs; uncertainty about our relationship was eating at us, devouring us and causing us to behave like children. We probably wanted to see how far we could push each other.

With one too many of these accusations, I snapped after a passionate argument and cut (very haphazardly) my long hair short, on one side of my head. I cried out: "You wanna accuse me of being a scarlet woman, I will carry the shame!" All very dramatic. I fled into the vineyards and cried my eyes out. This man was driving me crazy. When I finally calmed down and returned to the cottage, Peter had shaved all his hair off. We were ridiculous! I walked around with this hairdo for months. I wanted him to remember the false accusation. Of course I would have my moments as well, and accuse him of sordid trysts, which would end badly. Just thinking of all the energy we spent on this stupid jealousy... ugh, what was wrong with us?

We were in lust or in love or both. Peter would travel to Struisbaai, 3 hours away, to fish in a rock and surf competition... 10 hours of strenuous fishing. Immediately after the competition, he would drive all the way back to be with me. We were still keeping it a secret, and he could pinch a night off for us without too many questions asked. It wasn't our proudest moment, but there was a force between us that we could not contain.

Roger and Peter met and instantly liked each other. My son knew the truth and as is his nature, handled it with great understanding.

A GASSY SITUATION

Peter and I were invited to Selma's wedding up north, 12 hours of driving, and we saw a road trip on the horizon. Roger was busy with a paintball competition at the same time up north, and miraculously we planned to meet up there, with Michelle, his girlfriend flying in. Logistics of note. We eagerly set off in great anticipation of some time together. This was our first road trip and our first experience together as a couple. It presented a problem to me in the form of unwanted gas. Yip, you heard me. Gas. Building up in my tummy. I refused to let it rip. I was too shy. Can you believe it? So 7 hours into our road trip and I was in agony. I was curling in pain.
Now the farts were so comfortable they did not want to come out even if I was so inclined. We looked for a place to stay overnight. Peter wanted to spoil me with our first night and so we saw a lovely looking place that was pricey.

As I entered the bedroom, a large king size elaborate bed with drapery everywhere, in rich purples and emerald greens, was staring at us. Plump pillows and a beautiful plush duvet. The smell hit me. It was an other-worldly smell in the room. Evil. If Evil had a smell, this is what it would smell like.

I turned around, still in agony and we left. We found a National Parks chalet for the night.

By now it was clear to Peter that he had to intervene. I admitted to my folly. He subsequently laughed himself silly, poured me a warm bath and gently massaged the farts out of my tummy. He was definitely a keeper.

We met up with Roger, collected Michelle at the airport and joined the wedding party. Selma looked so beautiful... a very special day.

As the trip back was long, we decided to camp at Gariep Dam, sort of halfway towards home. Roger had arranged a tent for them and Peter and I had our own. No mattress, the bare essentials. It was only going to be for one night.

We found small fishing rods in the only little shop there was with the idea of spending the afternoon fishing. We eagerly put up camp. The tent that Roger had loaned from someone at the Waldorf School resembled a Bedouin tent with elaborate pieces of cloth going here and everywhere. No windows. I don't know how the tent was standing and in the middle of summer in the middle of the Karoo... hot, hot, hot. And Michelle, bless her soul, it was her first camping experience. She gave the tent one look and started looking for alternate accommodation, which she could not find as all the chalets were booked. She really was thrown into the deep end. And we were not very sympathetic. True to her nature, she decided fuckit, let me join in.

We fished, swam and braaied under the Karoo stars. Magical. The next morning we just could not face going home. We all agreed to stay another night. As we were not equipped and the shop had very little to offer (not even a cooler to keep things kind of cold), we bought loads and loads of ice in grocery bags and hung them in the trees.

With bags dripping all over the place, sauces and groceries strewn all over, we fished and cooked and had a ball. We did look like hillbillies. We agreed to stay another night. Peter and I sleeping on the hard ground. Funny enough, the shop had wonderful meat and I bought a huge chunk of fillet, about 4kg, and a block of cheese. A really big block of cheese. Peter made a concoction of sauces and marinated the fillet overnight. We lived off that fillet for days.

Roger and Michelle discovered night fishing and we stayed another night. Peter and I got sunstroke. He had his first army flashback while with me, a condition that soldiers suffer from when under stress. He had spent 4 years of his young life fighting a terrible Bush War in South Africa. The emotional scars visible now, years after the fact. We got over that and went on fishing. Eventually we decided we had to return and set off for the farm.

And so what was it that I smelled in that room that reminded me of evil? I do not know, but it made me think of an experience I had on the farm when Roger was about 3 years old.

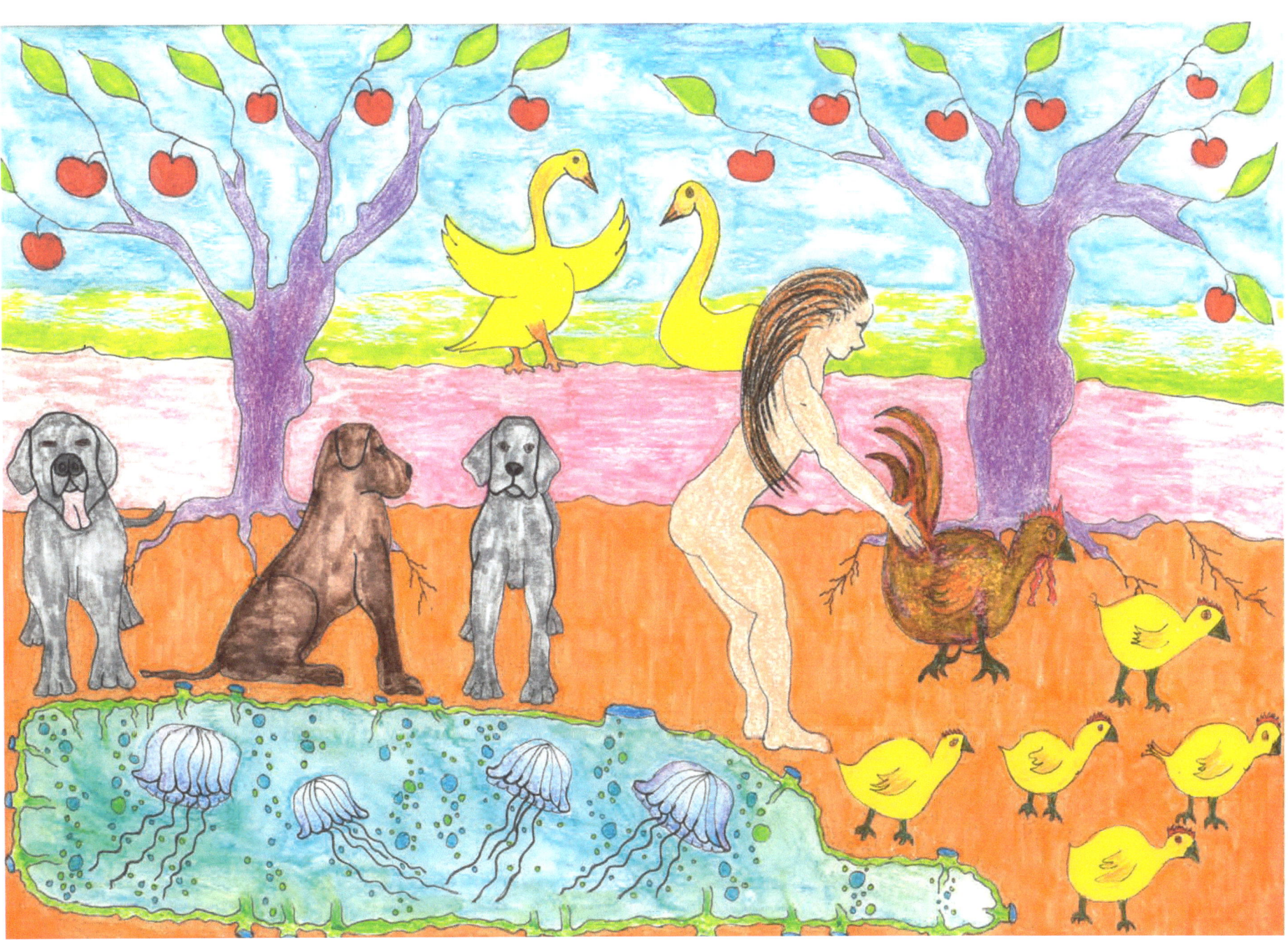

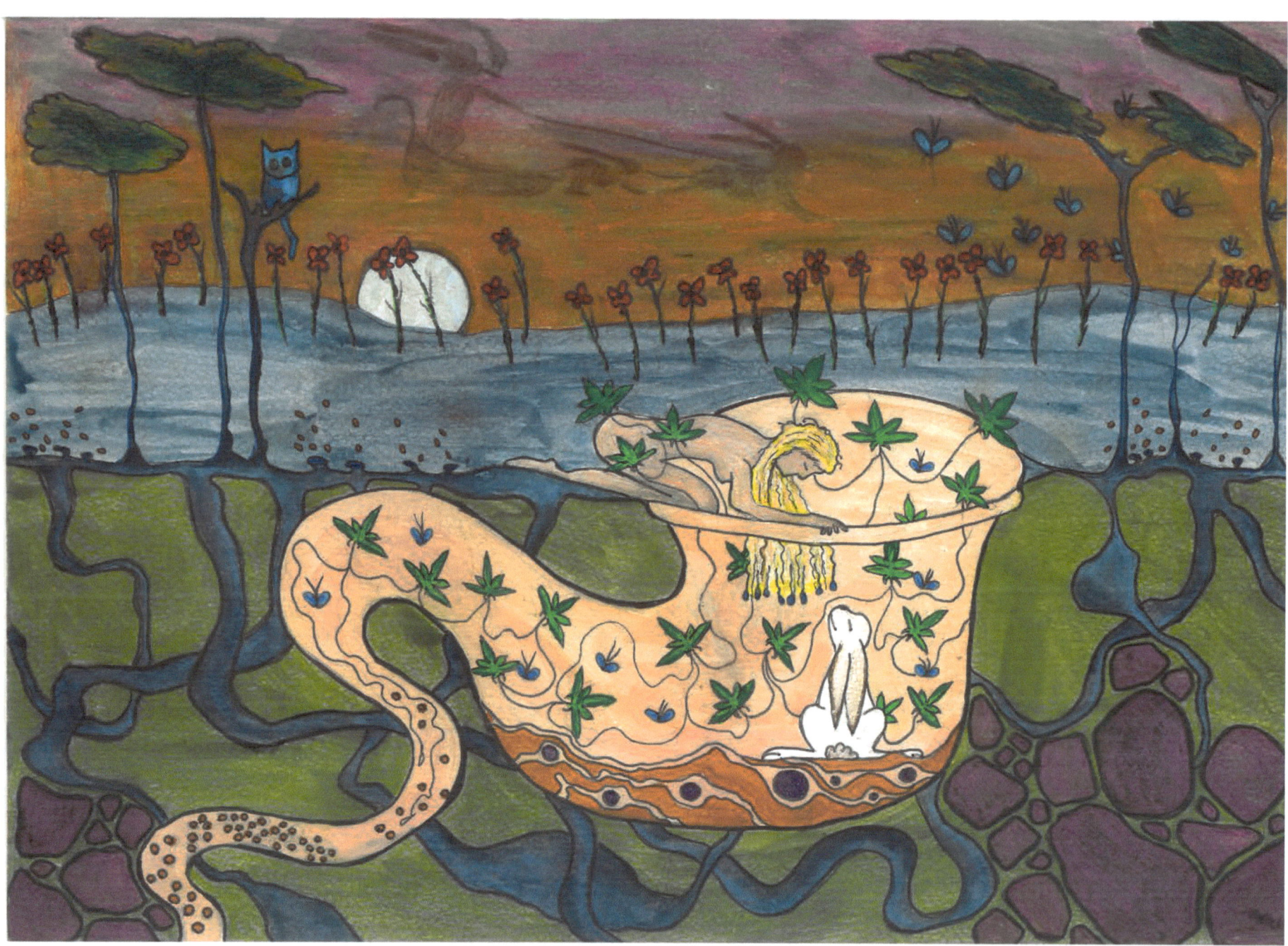

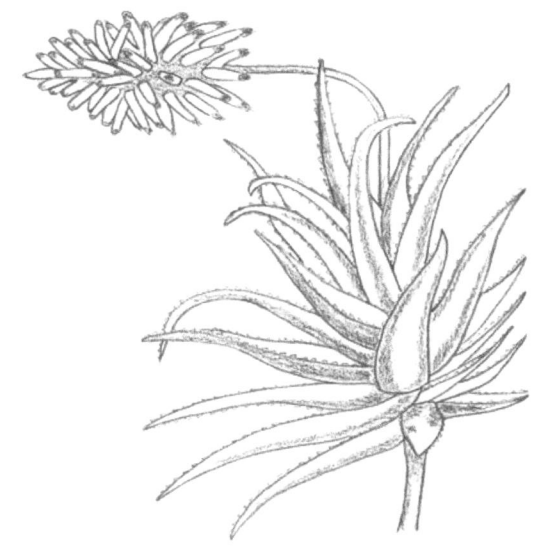

13
WHEN THINGS GET WEIRD

I had a paint technique business, and would find a lot of work for murals, which I could not fit in my busy schedule. I decided to find an artist whom I would commission for this work. I met up with Charlie. She was immensely talented, and in order to get to know her, I invited her and her boyfriend, Nick, to the farm for supper.
I set the table on our stoep (outside veranda), adding two very big, round candles, the size of soccer balls, as the only light on the stoep. We were so used to the dark that I never invested in proper lighting. It was all very haphazard in the house with the weirdest switches. To operate the passage light you would have to go to the kitchen, and the bedroom light was in the passageway.

We had a lovely meal with quite a bit of wine and Charlie went to lie down on the couch, a few meters away from where I was sitting with the freakin boyfriend on the stoep. Roger was fast asleep in my bed. Next thing is this boyfriend starts howling like a wolf. What? Did I just hear this man howl like a wolf? Were my ears going wonky on me? Nope there he howls again. And with Charlie fast asleep only meters away. So now he is throwing my cutlery into the bush behind him. He took off his shirt. Goodness me. And he is telling me what he wants to do with me. Pretty X-rated stuff.

He then took the big round candles and started dancing in a trance-like fashion, intermittently howling and talking dirty to me. What the fuck?

I picked up my senses and told him to go sleep with this girlfriend on the couch. My cutlery in the bushes. So I am not thinking straight. I

69

mean this is weird. No, it is past being weird. So, bright Anita locks herself in with this lunatic. I lock the front door. I go to my bedroom. Roger is ok. I cannot sleep.

I hear Charlie waking up, a geskarrel[30] taking place in the lounge... miraculously she found the front door key in the dark, door closing, car door, off they go. Thank fuck.

But now I cannot sleep. Something is not right. Now on the farm it is quiet. Every noise an animal makes, I can hear. It is deathly quiet. I know every noise in this house. Suddenly the doors of my kitchen cupboards start hitting open and closed. There was no mistaking the sound, and I was wide awake.

Now previously I had done work for a very religious couple. They belonged to one of those happy clappy churches. They were always preaching, seeing every opportunity as one to convert some unsus-pecting soul. In our conversations I had asked them as a point of interest, how they chase demons away.

I found them very interesting and their stories were intriguing. Their belief was so strong. The husband had a very bad back, and they went with me to pick guavas. He fell off the ladder. He was laying on the ground. He was badly injured and she healed him right there. I did see that.

So I took note of their method of chasing away demons, not thinking that I would ever use this information. For me it was just interesting.

Oh was I wrong.

That night with the doors banging open and closed... I did exactly what they had told me. I prayed with every part of my being and chased those demons out of my kitchen. They had told me that you have to chase them into something else, or they would be wandering around looking for other victims.

The only place I could think of was the sea, so it's possible that there are some demon sharks swimming around. Just saying. Immediately after chasing them off the farm, I fell asleep peacefully. The weirdest night of my life.

Next morning I was feeling a bit worried about Charlie with this freakin oke. I phoned her and she told me the following: When she woke up on the couch in my lounge, he was hissing like a snake. She knew a psychologist who lived in Stellenbosch, which was on their way home. Three o'clock in the morning she parked outside his house, and he had a look at her crazy boyfriend.

According to the psychologist, he was possessed by several demons. Months and months went by and I would feel a presence coming towards the farm, and whether it was my imagination or not, I was not going to take the chance. So I duly chased them away in the fashion that my clients had explained to me.

Charlie did a lot of work for me and I asked if her boyfriend had now been un-demoned. Yip, apparently so, so I invited them to join me on the farm. I had also invited some clients.

Well, you know it, but just as the party was getting going, this stupid boyfriend takes his shirt off, gets hold of the big round candles and starts doing this weird dance. This time I knew what was coming, and in front of everyone, I yelled at him to stop this immediately. You just stop this right now! I have no idea what everyone was thinking but he slotted back into his normal persona and we went on with the evening.

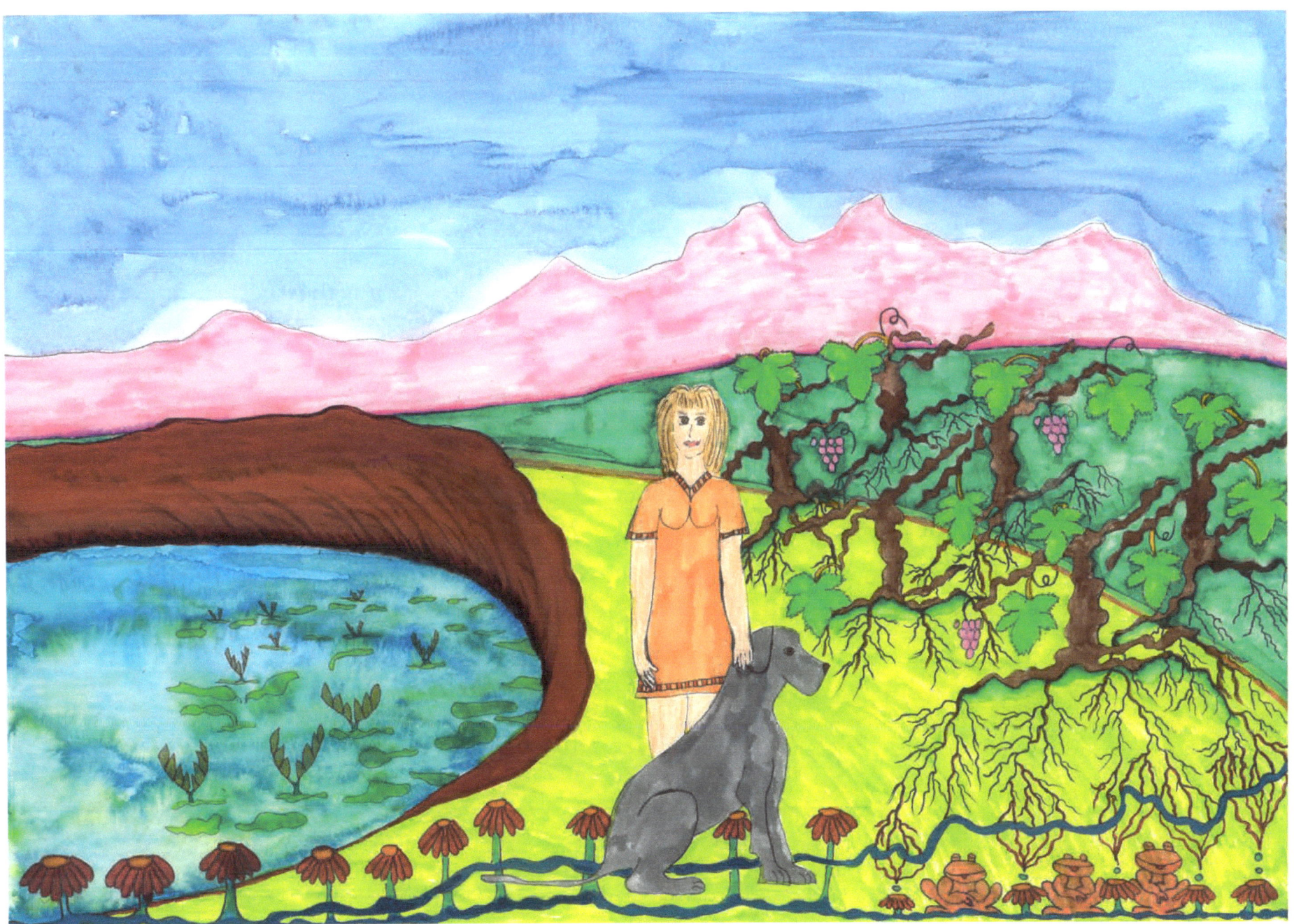

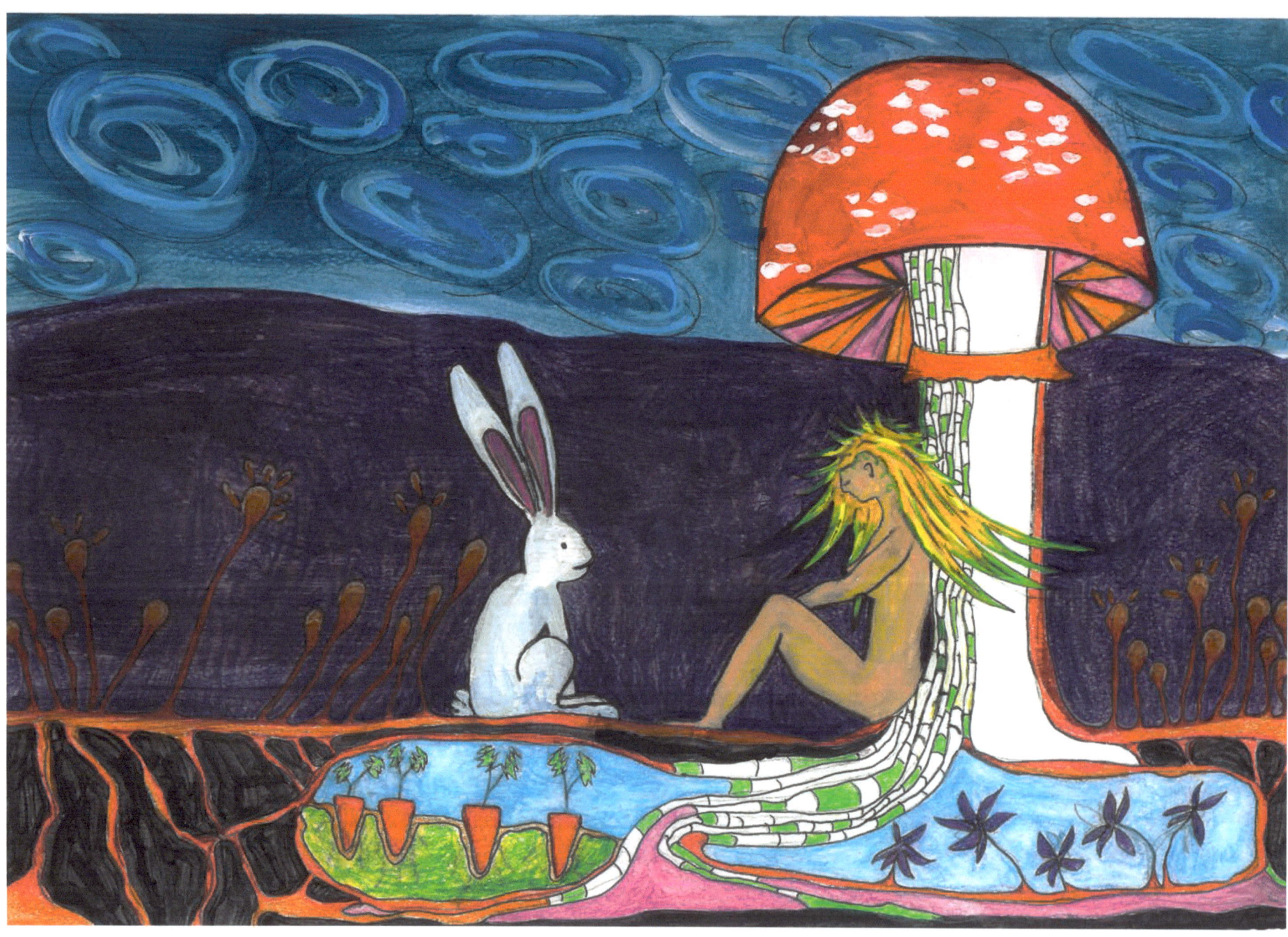

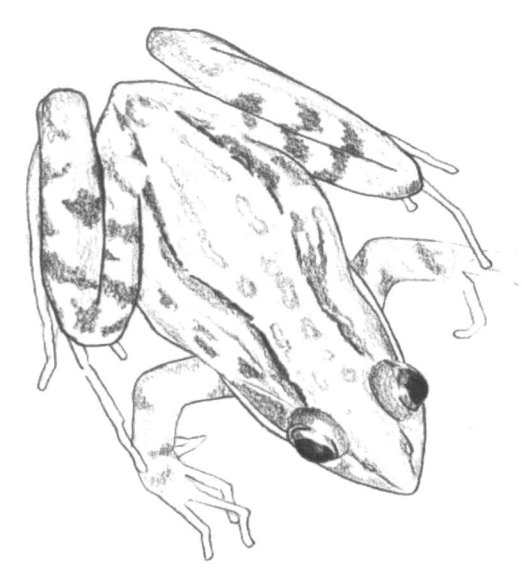

14

NEW CHAPTERS TO BE WRITTEN

Through all of the ups and downs, I kept gardening. I planted trees and shrubs around our little cottage reminiscent of the Voortrekker lagers[31] of my forefathers.

Now the house is invisible to the outside world and the birds just keep on coming. They rejoice in this jungle, and at one stage we stopped counting at 55 for the different bird species who would visit our haven. Frogs join the choir, an unusual amount of chameleons pull in. Everywhere, we have life in abundance.

Peter and I plonked a big old cast iron bath under our big palm with running hot and cold water. We would sit and dream for hours until our skin became 100 years old. Peter was busy with his divorce and he moved to the farm.

When 2017 hit, we faced the worst drought in South Africa that we had seen in many decades.

SEASONS, CYCLES AND SONS
BOLANDER, 29 MARCH 2017

So, 2017 has been packed with interesting events, happenings, decisions and circumstances. We are not even halfway through the year, and I feel constantly in need of a drink.

My family was in a holding pattern for a while. My son and his girlfriend were studying, with all they had to pass their Cambridge exams: my life partner battling with work and money, myself bitterly unhappy in my daily employment.

And then 2017 happened. My son and his girlfriend are dispersing to two opposite corners of America, my partner started his own business again, and I found happy employment with an old boss.

The four of us recently stood at the southernmost tip of Africa; such a symbolic, special place. We took a selfie of our feet, standing at this most beautiful spot we call Africa – every one of us on the precipice of new beginnings. It was quite mind-blowing.

So off my beloved Roger goes. To his birthplace... America. Maybe never to return, and if so, just for a visit. Maybe? Who knows?

My cousin called me: 'Your heart must be in pieces?"

My response: "No"

For 21 years I prepared my son for just this event. That moment when he makes that crucial decision: "I need to make my own life" I didn't have to kick him out. No coaxing. No threats. Just a realisation that life beckons... and when you're young, strong and confident, failure is not an option. No, my heart is relieved.

Her retort: "But it must have been really hard raising him on your own?"

No! It was a privilege. To not have to consider another opinion, to have carte blanche in all decisions. What a unique opportunity... a huge responsibility yes, but a complete, 100% privilege.
And now my job is done and my life can continue. New beginnings, new opportunities, new discoveries and a dizzying freedom.
So, enough about empty nests... I feel so parched. My garden is just giving up. I can't handle this drought anymore. I feel like I am drying out. As if I am in sync with my withering vegetables. Parched beyond endurance.

When I walk up my path barefoot on my once lush, green and now non-existing lawn, I feel like one of those 150-year-old tortoises with the accompanying leathery skin, slowly making my way up my prickly, dry and dead pathway.

Water! Water! Please, I am so thirsty. I really do need a drink. When it starts raining, I will be the crazy woman next to the highway dancing in the rain. So just smile and wave please.

I belong to a gardening club on Facebook, and what I love is that there are people with no experience, people who can quote scientific names, people with years of experience and people who have just discovered their passion.

So to one such person I responded: "When you start referring to your garden in the third person... when you feel her pulse.... when you suffer her thirst... delight in her generosity... understand that she feeds many creatures, not just you.... then you are truly in love." I congratulated her and said that I am celebrating my 20th anniversary.

It made me think. When you are a gardener, then you are in a relationship with your garden. It is akin to a marriage. The ups and downs, the hard work, the rewards.

And next season all starts again. A never-ending cycle. I wrote a poem to help with my son leaving. It goes something like this:

DIE KIND

(I always referred to him as just that)
Hy loop hier uit, sonner bagasie,
Sak en pak die toekoms in
Ligte voetspore, skaars n duik in die hede
Die verlede haal sy krom vinger uit
21 jaar van koester, van lewenslesse leer
Sy krom vinger krap in my hart en grawe twyfel uit
Die kind moet die toekoms bloots ry
Want tyd vir opsaal is maar min
Van klein tyd gesweis aan my, n stuk bloudraad hou ons vas
Leer en lag, trane van skade en trots,
Toekoms haal sy bliksker uit
Die bloudraad nou net n goue draad

THE CHILD

(Roughly translated by Carolyn Frost)
He walks away, carrying no luggage
Towards the future, he holds all he has
Light footprint, barely a dent in the present
The past takes out his crooked Finger
21 years of nurturing, life lessons learned
The child must mount the future bareback
No time for saddling up
Welded to my body from youngest day, we are bonded by a piece
of thick wire
Learning and laughing, tears from wounds and pride
Future reveals his shears
The thick wire is now just a golden thread.

STRIVING TOWARDS SELF-SUSTAINABILITY

Never afraid of failure, I tried my hand at exotic vegetables. Composting and soil health became a passion and by now I knew what I was doing. The size of my vegetables were directly linked to the care I took in creating the perfect growing conditions.

Each spring we would harvest an abundance of asparagus, and artichokes became an ordinary vegetable. Someone gave me a curry leaf tree as a gift and I set out to grow everything you would need to make your own curry paste. I planted ginger, garlic and lemon grass and stumbled upon turmeric roots while on a holiday with my sister when they were visiting from Australia.

I stuck it in the ground, and 5 years later it produced its first exotic bloom, quite unexpected, as I had no clue of the nature of turmeric. I stopped buying at the shops and my enthusiasm soared. I kept on adding gardens. My fool-proof method of rehabilitating hard, clay soil I refined to an art form. And patience was a big part of the success.

The first year I would plant mielies[32]. It is an aggressive grower with an impressive root system. I would top-dress with compost at the beginning of the growing cycle. We would harvest so much corn that sharing with friends and family would be essential. Of course our ever growing birdlife took full advantage of the abundance.

After the summer I would chop the mielies half way and leave the roots in the soil, breaking up the hard clay as it decomposes. My next crop fitting it in just before autumn, would be green beans, a nitrogen fixer and a wonderful vegetable to eat. The soil becomes richer with microbial life. Adding compost with every new crop then ensures years and years of great harvests.

KINDRED SPIRITS

Fishing was a sport I always enjoyed. Mostly boat angling with some river fishing when I was growing up. Living close to the Atlantic and Indian oceans, we always joined in the annual crayfish season. I knew nothing of rock and surf fishing. But Peter does.

I begged him to teach me. It is a male-dominated sport with very few female anglers. He's a member of a very masculine fishing club so it took some convincing. It happened. With great patience he has taught me about a very technical sport. Bait presentation, casting, knots which I still struggle with, the ability to read water, the list is endless. I now stand by him side by side, 10 hrs of fishing no matter the weather – howling South-Easter wind, rain, bitterly cold days. We fish!
Our favourite place to visit is the Orange River near Vioolsdrif. We camp often in the nature reserve with nothing much but food, a tent and fishing gear.

And we fish. Huge big and small mouth yellows (indigenous fresh water fish), big ole barbers[33], which is a favourite of mine to catch. So how are the two of us today?

We are doing exceptionally well. Weathering retrenchments, Covid-19 and birthing a new business, Magic Rabbit Compost.
It happened as all things happen on the farm. A friend, Gordon, asked if we would be interested in keeping rabbits. Seeing an alternative meat source I asked if they were meat rabbits. "Of course they are," our friend replied. Of course they were not. We kept them anyway and started the interesting journey of understanding rabbits.

Eagerly setting out to build a cage for them, not completely understanding how crafty they are. Numerous escapes later saw Peter building a simple trap which we used quite effectively. We would see a rabbit in the vineyards... but was that not the one we caught yesterday. Fuckit, it is! We slaughtered them all. But the idea of a very healthy meat alternative kept us interested, and after a lot of Googling, we decided to purchase our first three New Zealand whites, a large meat breed.

Rabbits are surprisingly difficult to keep, especially if you want to keep them in a free-range scenario. We have never liked the idea of caged animals, and have always made sure that our camps are large, so whatever we keep can do their thing in relatively big surroundings. And the carrot that Bugs Bunny loves? That is the biggest lie. Too much sugar. Rabbits have very sensitive digestive tracts. They cannot vomit, so have a one-way only type of scenario. If that gets blocked, instant death. That sounds a bit dramatic, but they get GI stasis and bloat up like a balloon, and then they die. So their diet is all important, and keeping them regular and flatulence free, so to speak, is of utmost importance.

I had been using the rabbit dropping in the vegetable gardens and saw phenomenal results – and the idea of a lifelong dream, became a reality. I researched rabbit manure, the little bit that is out there, and discovered real black gold. Magic Rabbit Compost was born during our lockdown (check out https://magicrabbit.co.za/).

We continue to fight for soil health, organic produce, sustainability which lies close to our hearts. We are living our dream. Nobody else's dream but ours. We have the same disregard for other people's opinions on the way we choose to live.

This is our time now.

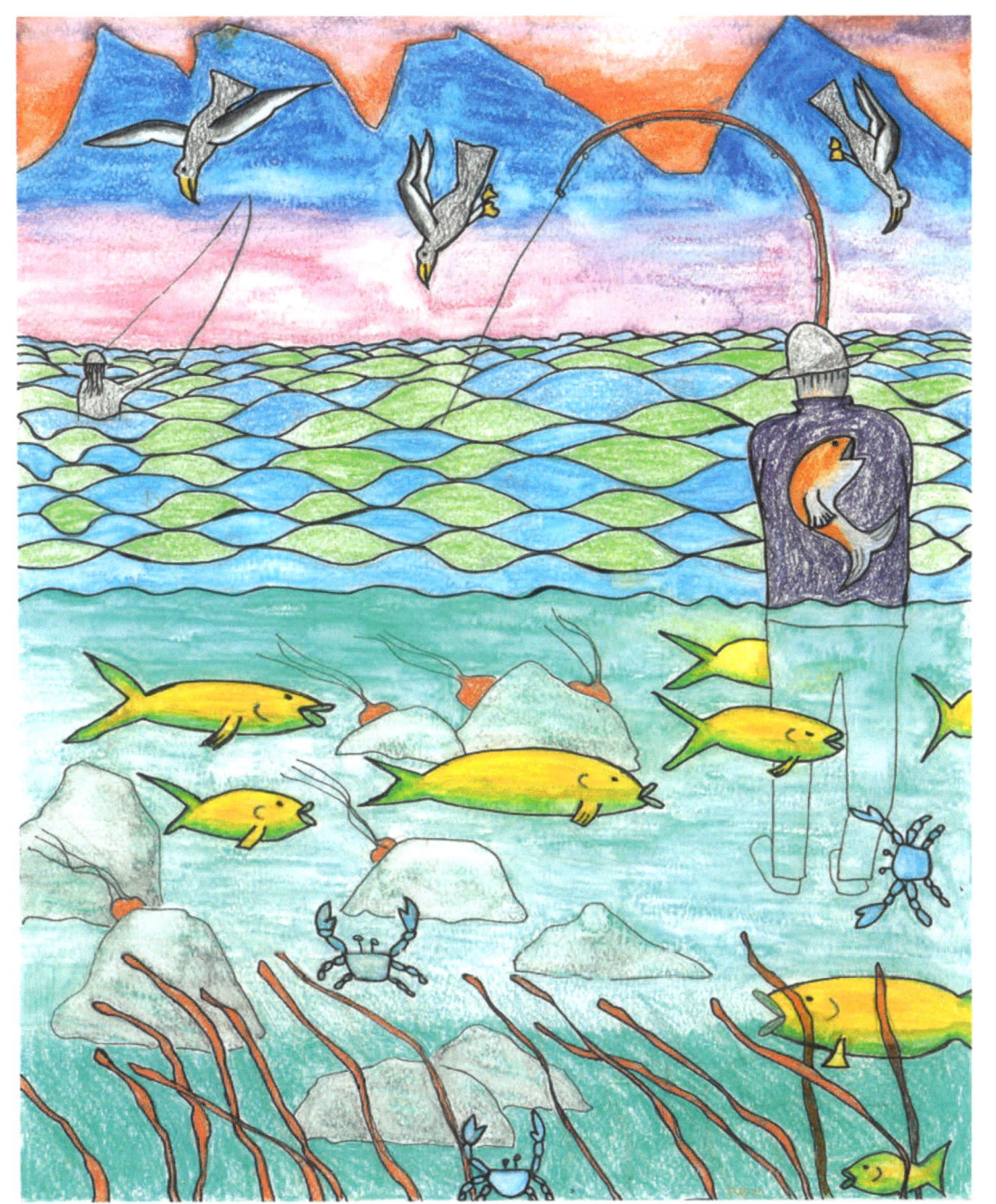

Glossary of Terms

1. *Shasta daisies:* Leucanthemum Superbum. Fancy for huge daisies

2. *Lorrie:* A big 10 ton truck

3. *Beginsels:* Principles

4. *Snoek:* Thyrsites Atun, a very large, thin silver fish caught off the West Coast of South Africa

5. *Bakkie:* Pickup truck

6. *Maermerries:* Shins

7. *Sonneblom:* Sunflower

8. *Mielies:* Corn

9. *Kakking out:* A very bad tongue lashing containing many expletives

10. *Spit braai:* Rotisserie barbeque

11. *Stoep:* Back porch

12. *Kak difficult:* As in extremely

13. *Boerpampoen:* Cucurbita Maxima. A very big round, white, flattish pumpkin

14. *Waterblommetjies:* Aponogeton Distachyos, an edible, wild water plant

15. *Potjie:* A very traditional cast iron pot used for fire cooking

16. *Helderberg:* Mountain range close to the farm

17. *Om't ewe:* Either way

18. *Swetterjoel:* Just a whole lot

19. *Bundu Bashing:* The African Bush

20. *jy moet hieruit:* Flippin' get out of my tummy!

21. *Spekboom:* Portulacaria Afra, a native plant that utilizes abnormal quantities of carbon dioxide to produce an unusual amount of oxygen

22. *Harde gat:* A very special type of stubborn

23. *Blertse:* It's a unique Afrikaans word that I have no idea how to translate. It's the action but linked to a sound a Muscovy makes when pooping

24. *Lekkerbek:* Foodie

25. *Koekenaap:* A really small rural town in the middle of nowhere and somewhere.

26. *Braaier:* The person that barbeques... a sacred duty amongst South Africans

27. *Boerewors:* A traditional South African sausage made with beef and pork fat

28. *Sewende Laan:* A popular television soapie about people living and working on a street in Hillbrow, Johannesburg, where everyone knew everyone's business

29. *Tamelejie:* A really sticky mess

30. *Geskarrel:* Sounds of disorganized movement

31. *Voortrekkers:* My forefathers that fucked off and moved into the interior of South Africa were called Voortrekkers. As a means of defending a very vulnerable exodus with livestock, woman and children, they pulled their ox wagons in a circle, which was called a lager

32. *Mielies:* Corn

33. *Barber:* Clarias Gariepinus. South African catfish

www.ingramcontent.com/pod-product-compliance
Lightning Source LLC
Chambersburg PA
CBHW041110170526
45159CB00009BA/2907